Mystic Visions:
Black Elk's Great Vision Clarified

Mystic Visions:

Black Elk's Great Vision Clarified

Quentin H. Young

Winfield, IL, USA
2017

First Edition 2015
Printed in the USA
Second Edition 2017
Printed in the USA

Cover illustration © 2017 Ginger Young
Photos © 2015 Ginger Young

Permission can be obtained for re-use of portions of material by writing to the address below. Some permission requests can be granted free of charge, others carry a fee.

Mystic Visions Publishing
PO Box 462
Winfield IL 60190

mysticvisions26@aol.com
http://mysticvisions.world

Library of Congress Control Number: 2017905899
ISBN-13: 978-0692879689
ISBN-10: 0692879684

Quentin H. Young has accomplished for me what no other author has ever been able to do. For the first time in my many attempts to understand Black Elk's vision, I have an understanding thanks to Young's breakdown of the vision. Paragraph by paragraph the vision is broken down into understandable bits, like devouring a great lunch one morsel at a time. Added to the information are the tidbits from Young's own life and visions, making it a personal story as well as a story that history is still searching answers for.

Young's great descriptive phrasing of his visions took me with him, giving answers about why one Sun Dances or seeks a vision quest. Not a holy book, but a human book, making sense and explaining many Lakota terms and customs I never had the privilege of knowing. An exciting read, full of humor, spirit and the interpretation of a knowledgeable man willing to share his own visions as well as that of Black Elk. This book is for those who wish to understand Black Elk's Great Vision, the spirituality behind it, and an insight as to why modern man still seeks visions, and where these visions may take him or her.

~ *Sharon Hogue, Society Editor -*
Menominee News, Retired.

Quentin H. Young has helped put the breath of life into the vision of the great holy man Black Elk. I do believe Black Elk's spirit must have given him guidance and inspiration.

I only hope the reader will be touched by this knowledge and understanding of how we can all, together, dance under the great Tree of Life as one people within the sacred hoop. Then, the vision of Black Elk would come as a beautiful sunrise and bring a new re-creation to humanity. Thank you, my friend.

We are all related.

~ *Chief Steve McCullough, Salt-Creek Sun Dance.*

I dedicate this book to all the people of the world seeking balanced spirituality, and to my wife Ginger, for her encouragement, belief in me over the years, and selfless act of giving up vacations and weekends, so I could follow the Lakota spiritual way of life and write this book.

Acknowledgments

To my dear friends, Dan Creely Jr. for writing the foreword and who is known as "the Connector" of like-minded people and encouraged me to finish this book. To Sharon Hogue, a wise woman who encouraged me to write in-depth about my own experiences. I thank Melissa Rutkowski and my wife Ginger for helping with the original editing of this book. I also thank Kathy Stoops, who coaxed me onto the 'good red road', Chief Steve McCullough, and Earl Meshiguad for their teachings. It is with fond memory and gratitude to the late Dr. James (Jim) E. Gillihan, the late Vernal Cross Sr., the late Olivia Black Elk Pourier and the late Charles Fast Horse for their teachings. I would also like to thank all the elders who have shared their sacred way of life with me over the many years. Finally, I would like to thank my Mother Rose Mary, Grandmother Rose Leaf Eliot, and Great Grandmother Eliza Milton for holding onto our Lakota heritage.

Foreword

Imagine if you felt like you were attached to an invisible umbilical cord pulling you along to an unseen destination for your entire life. You could not see where you were being led but you knew you were on the right path ... a path with a heart. You knew you were being guided to do something. Then, after 40 years of study, dedication, and participation in Lakota ceremonies, you felt your work was nearly completed only to discover at 68 years old, it had only just begun; you were able to look back on your life's path and you could see where they, "the spirits", had guided you in EVERYTHING leading you to this moment in your life. They have been preparing you to do something meaningful.

Based on the compelling vision of Nicolas Black Elk as written by John G. Neihardt in *Black Elk Speaks*, Quentin H. Young has unlocked its messages, as he clarifies each detail of the vision. A vision given for all people of the world then, now, and for the future, and explains why a vision given to a young Lakota boy in 1872 has relevance today.

Readers will find this book historical in nature and culturally enlightening. Quentin stated, "I believe a vision given to Black Elk, a great Lakota Holy Man in 1872, is now being clarified so it can help heal the world." He goes on to explain the ancient Lakota worldview so people not familiar with the Lakota spiritual way of life can grasp and understand the meaning, importance and depth behind Black Elk's Great Vision.

Quentin shares his personal and incredible journey of his life on the 'good red road', listening to spirit since 1950. His own experiences and Black Elk's Great Vision are woven together throughout this book, *Mystic Visions: Black Elk's Great Vision Clarified.* You will read how "the spirits" connected the invisible umbilical cord to him and gently guided, tugged, protected and pulled him along the path on his own journey. Quentin shares how the elders and teachers he needed, and the experiences appeared at exactly the right moment.

In *Mystic Visions: Black Elk's Great Vision Clarified*, Quentin provides his insights, understanding, and clarification of Black Elk's Great Vision in a unique and easily digestible format. His forensic examination breaks down the major points of the Great Vision, sentence by sentence, and section by section. Quentin is the first to put dates based on the historical time-periods of the four 'ascents', referred to as "generations". He begins with the year 1863 and guides us through the occurrences in each of the four ascents. You will find Quentin's writing is as the circular narrative style used in Native culture to share stories. One piece leads to the next, then to the next, and then it comes back to where it began.

I recall a Pottawatomie Elder, Nowaten Dale Thomas, once shared that people search their entire lives to find spirit. What they do not realize is, you cannot find spirit, spirit finds you, and then you need to listen. Spirit found Quentin in 1973 when 'IT' told him, "you will pick up the pipe" and he has been listening ever since.

Grandmother Keewaydinoquay, an Ojibwa Elder, and traditional Herbalist and I were sitting quietly at my kitchen table. She reached into an old beaded leather bag she carried on her person, slowly pulled out a complete canine tooth from an adult black bear, gently placed it on the table in front of me, and said it is my major medicine piece. She spoke deliberately and slowly to make sure I listened to the teaching. This tooth is much like all situations in life. There is much more involved than what is merely exposed on the surface. Black Elk's vision is like the Bear's tooth: there is much more to the vision than what appears on the surface.

Quentin had many elders and teachers in his life; one of them was Dr. James (Jim) E. Gillihan, (1935 - 2002). He was a registered member of the Cherokee, appointed in 1972, as the director of the Natural History museum of the University of South Dakota. He would visit Lakota elders as part of his work, and was recognized as a man with good intentions and a good heart. They taught him their language, traditions, and ceremonies in the Lakota/Dakota way of life.

In 1991, Dr. Gillihan became one of Quentin's teachers, teaching him many of the Lakota traditions. He trusted and respected Quentin for the path he walks as a friend, a student of Lakota culture, a spiritual leader, and a warrior for peace for the ongoing of the people, but most importantly, a person with a good heart.

In 1995, Dr. Gillihan sponsored Quentin as a Sun Dancer, and guided him to the Salt Creek Sun Dance in southern Indiana.

Vernal Cross, a medicine man from Pine Ridge, South Dakota traveled to Indiana and served as the intercessor to the Sun Dance in 1996 & 1997. Vernal had the authority to shut down a Sun Dance if things were not right. Steve McCullough shared a story about when Vernal arrived the first year at the Sun Dance grounds, he saw a man sitting in the (Sun Dance) tree. To Vernal, this was a good thing; the spirits were blessing the dance.

In 1997, Quentin, along with several other people, heard Vernal share the reason he traveled to Indiana to oversee the dance. he believed the Salt Creek Sun Dance was the extension of Black Elk's Great Vision. The man (spirit) sitting in the tree was the validation for his beliefs. Black Elk's vision is to bring every color of man together from the four quarters of the world to the flowering tree to heal the hoop of the nation/world.

Quentin Sun Danced from 1996 to 1999, and has been serving as a Sun Dance helper to the intercessor, from 2000 through 2016

Dr. Gillihan demonstrated to me the four qualities of a Lakota warrior namely: bravery, fortitude, generosity, and wisdom. Dr. Gillihan introduced me to Quentin in 1995, and I have had the opportunity to observe him closely in many, many different situations, and have observed Quentin walk-his-talk every time with integrity. This is the reason I agreed to write the foreword to, *Mystic Visions: Black Elks Great Vision Clarified.*

Dan Creely Jr. Professor Emeritus, Northeastern Illinois University

Table of Contents

Preface

I was not born on a Lakota reservation, as a mix blood Lakota, I had to seek out my connection to the Lakota people. Since 1973, I have been fortunate to have had traditional Lakota elders (teachers), medicine men and spirits help me to understand the Lakota spiritual way of life and the metaphysical with respect to how it relates to visions like that of Nicholas Black Elk.

One of the advantages I had in writing this book is that I had one foot in the world of the Lakota, and the other foot in the non-Indian world. When studying Black Elk's vision, I had to think like a Lakota person, and then write this book as a non-Indian for people not familiar with the Lakota spiritual way of life. In doing so, I hope the reader can get a better glimpse into both worlds, as I truly believe this vision is for the people of the world.

Since 1990, I have studied Black Elk's vision of the nation's hoop and the flowering tree as told through the writing of John G. Neihardt's *Black Elk Speaks*. Over the years, I have spent countless hours trying to present Black Elk's vision in a forum people not familiar with the Lakota spiritual way of life could relate. In 1998 and for the next seven years I lectured at the College of DuPage, Illinois, a three-hour accredited course in Social Science called "Native Americans and their Mystic Visions."

In 2005 thru 2008, I offered the same course off campus. I have also guest lectured at North Central College, Northeastern Illinois, Northwestern, DePaul, and Southern Illinois Universities.

Due to the complexity of Black Elk's vision, it will require a forensic look at its content. This book looks closely at Black Elk's vision, to understand how it played out for the indigenous people and the Europeans that settled on the North American continent and the world as a whole. In this book, I was able to create a timeline, using the historic record for each of the four ascents referred to as generations. It also offers the reader a better understanding of the American Indians way of thinking; this thinking is what sets the American Indians visions apart from hallucinations.

Some names were changed in this book to protect their anonymity.

Quentin H Young
Winfield Illinois, January 2016

Chapter 1: Prologue

This book offers a clarification of Nicholas Black Elk's Great Vision from Chapter 3 of *Black Elk Speaks*, by John G. Neihardt, The Complete Edition, 2014 University of Nebraska Press. It is with the deepest respect for John G. Neihardt, Nicholas Black Elk and his great vision, I feel drawn to offer a clarification of this vision for the reader.

One of the first lessons I learned from the Lakota is that it is not appropriate to speak of another person's vision. In doing so, we take their vision as though it was our own to share. What sets Nicholas Black Elk's vision apart from others is he shared his vision of the sacred hoop and flowering tree with John G. Neihardt, thus giving his permission to place it into the book entitled *Black Elk Speaks*. Therefore, Black Elk gave this vision to all future generations thus, allowing us to evaluate and speak freely of this magnificent vision.

If you have not had the opportunity to read the book, *Black Elk Speaks*, I strongly suggest you pick up a copy. It is an historic look into the life and times of the great Holy Man Black Elk an Oglala (To scatter one's own) Lakota (Sioux) and his Great Vision.

The following is a summary account from, John G. Neihardt's, *Black Elk Speaks*, Chapter 1 The Offering of the Pipe.

Black Elk:

Black Elk said his winters (life) were not much to write about, even though it bends him like a heavy snow. The great vision and struggle the Lakota would endure during his life was worth telling, so he agreed to give his story to John G. Neihardt.

Clarification:

Like Black Elk, I do not think my personal life (winters) is much to talk about. My draw to the Lakota spiritual way of life is worth explaining. Before I begin the explanation of Black Elk's Great Vision, I will share some of my experiences, visions and phenomenal occurrences. Throughout this book, I interlace my personal visions and experiences, which parallel much of what Black Elk spoke of in the book, *Black Elk Speaks*.

In doing so, I hope to give some credence to what Black Elk spoke of in his Great Vision of the sacred hoop and flowering tree. My intention is to help the reader find clarity with respect to what a vision is, how one receives visions, and the method of deciphering them.

Visions do not come to us gift wrapped with fancy bows; they are symbolic with respect to the individual receiving them. A personal vision given to an individual might have a different meaning for another person depending on his or her spiritual needs. Most of the time, personal visions are as signposts helping us make changes in our lives so we can be inservice to others.

Black Elk's Great Vision was a world vision, not meant for just one individual, but for the whole of humanity. As we get further into Black Elk's vision, this will become apparent.

My Personal Journey

Jump

From 1962 through 1965, I served as a paratrooper in the US Army's 101st Airborne. I first realized there was some kind of a spirit intervention in 1962 at age 18 while attending Jump School at Fort Benning, Georgia. To obtain paratrooper wings we are required to make five jumps. While making my third jump, I injured my left knee thus requiring the use of crutches for the next two weeks. At the end of the two weeks, the Jump

Commander said, "If you do not make the forth jump tomorrow, you will be washed out of jump school and sent to a leg group (regular army)." It was my desire to earn my wings so, the following morning, I discarded the crutches and strapped on a parachute.

While limping toward the plane, a C-119, a corporal pulled me out of line and said, "The post General wants to see you." By this time, I was quite upset as, I had never seen or talked to a General before. I entered his office and made the best salute I could conjure up under the circumstances. He asked me, "Why are you limping?" and then went on to say, "If you are injured, you should not try to make this jump." I crossed my fingers and told him my foot fell asleep, and it was feeling much better now. Looking at me over his glasses he said, "Dismissed, and do not walk out of here limping, or you can take that chute off!"

Biting my lip, I exited his office with a steady stride until I made it inside the waiting plane. I must have used every puke bag Uncle Sam had on the plane, as I was scared sick. The pain was horrible, but I was determined to earn my wings. Therefore, I just sat there thinking everything will be fine. When the Jump Commander gave the signal to stand and hook up, my stomach dropped to my feet. I hooked my static line to the cable running from the rear of the plane to the front. The static line is a fifteen-foot-long strap we attach to a cable inside the plane. The other end is weaved into the backside of the parachute pack that pulls the parachute out and breaks loose, after the person jumping clears the plane.

I began thinking, 'How the heck am I going to make this jump?' Then, the Jump Commander gave the order for the men at the rear of the plane to stand in the door. At this point, I decided it was all over. When I reached the rear of the plane, my decision was to step out of line and refuse to jump. That was my plan, but as plans go, I made a hard left and jumped through the open door with the rest of my class. I kept putting my left foot on top of my right foot and then would say to myself, 'What are you trying to do, break your right leg, as well?' When we are about fifty feet from the ground, you are supposed to look at the horizon, point your toes, and wait for the ground. In those days, we were sinking at about eighteen feet a second so the landing was a bit rough. It is like running and jumping off a 12-foot high roof.

The parachute landing fall (PLF) is repeated daily during jump school, until our landing becomes automatic, without our even thinking about it. One lands on the balls of their feet twists to the left or right contacting the ground with the side of the calf, the side of upper thigh, the glute and finally the upper part of the torso just behind the shoulder, the lat. If it is a windy day, you could end up repeating this move across the ground a couple of times.

Hanging in the chute I waited for the ground to finish me off when, I noticed my fellow jumpers hit the ground with their chutes breaking and falling all around them. Finally, I looked down only to notice my feet were about three inches up off the ground just hanging there. I looked up expecting to find my chute caught in a tree, only to find it fully deployed, breathing in and out. As my feet slowly touched, I laid back onto the ground, as if someone was holding my hands.

At that moment, my feelings were surreal as, I watched my chute break and fall to the ground; updrafts do not occur this close to the ground. Not understanding what had just happened from this soft landing, I felt it defied reality and began looking for a spirit named God. The point in all this is something mysterious was going on; I most certainly needed help on that day and it showed up. It is a time in my life I will always remember, a time when I flew with spirits.

A few days later, my knee had healed well enough to make my fifth jump. Upon landing, I bounced as hard and high as the next person did without causing any further damage to my knee. Assigned to the 101st Airborne after graduating from jump school, I would make another 34 jumps bouncing hard every time. There were two exceptions with respect to the hard landings, one jump in the early afternoon where the Air Force managed to drop us into trees, and one nighttime jump when again they managed to drop us into trees. In both cases, I made it through the trees without injury, with my chute caught in the top of a tree and my heels just touching the ground. Talk about a standing landing.

The Journey Begins

In the late summer of 1973 at 29 years old, my personal journey on the 'red road', the Lakota spiritual way of life was about to begin. While sitting on the floor in my home in San Antonio, Texas during a deep meditation something strange happened. Two spirits came into the room and sat down across from me. At the time, if I had just been sitting around, I would have been startled at the sight of them. For some reason, I was not upset by their presence; it was what they had to say that scared the fire out of me. This is what they said; *You will pick up the peace pipe (caŋnuŋpa) and seek out/or go to the Lakota to learn how to carry it. When you learn how to carry the pipe in the traditional way, you will begin to teach people how to reverse the negative.*

Startled, I jumped to my feet saying, 'I cannot do this.' The vision of the two spirits faded away, leaving me alone in the room. You see, back then, I did not care for people, and teaching them anything was not in my plans. I knew nothing about reversing the negative or the Lakota and even less about the pipe. I was the fourth generation of my mother's people, the Lakota. (See Figure 1 and 2) My family had no idea how to reconnect with these Lakota and neither did I. For the next fifteen years, I thought I had avoided getting involved in this pipe thing. What I would learn over those years is spirits do not usually mean 'right now'.

In 1977, four years after my vision, I began to have a strong desire to learn more about the Lakota, and why the two spirits from my vision came to me. As a mixed-blood, not growing up on the reservation, I lacked any true knowledge of the Lakota spiritual ways and most notably, I lacked any real power (spiritual understanding).

Figure 1: Rose Leaf Eliot, my Sicangu Lakota Grandmother with my Mother Rose Mary, taken some time in July 1918. Rose Leaf married Clarence Likens, and they had one child, my mother Rose Mary Likens.

Figure 2: Eliza Milton, my Great Grandmother, 1854-1941. Eliza was a full blood Sicangu Lakota borne in 1854 in Nebraska. In 1855, a soldier took Eliza from the battlefield of the Blue Water Fight and gave her to the Milton's of Missouri. Soon after, Eliza was adopted by them and raised as a white. She married James Eliot and had seven children, six girls and one boy. It was said that wherever James and Eliza traveled the whites called him a squaw man.
(a derogatory statement)

It was on a warm day in June 1977, when my eleven-year-old son Jeff, his step mother and I set out for the Rosebud Reservation located in South Dakota. We drove through the Reservation stopping at the small town of St Francis and visited a small Lakota Museum. After a pleasant visit at the museum, we set out to find a place to camp for the night. It was getting late so we elected to camp at a rest area having just one picnic table. Rather than taking the time to set up a tent, we chose to spend the night in my 1976 Ford Courier pickup, equipped with a small camper top.

The next morning at the picnic table, potato and egg tacos were being prepared on our camp stove, when from out of nowhere came an elderly Indian man walking toward us from out of the West. I should have seen him coming for quite a distance, as the terrain in that area was relatively flat. He greeted us with a broad smile and said, "Good morning" and inquired as to where we were from. For some reason, I felt compelled to share with him the story of my mother's family and why I came to the Rosebud. With a smile, he said, "Welcome home." I asked if he would like to join us for breakfast and he said, "Yes please, it really smells good."

After breakfast and a short visit, the elder stood up and thanked us for the fine breakfast, bid us farewell and continued his journey toward the East. I turned back toward the picnic table to pick up the dishes, and when I turned back toward the direction he had gone, he was now where to be seen. This elder vanished as quickly as he had appeared; leaving me perplexed. Where did he come from and where the heck did he go? Come to think about it, I did not even get his name.

After we left the Rosebud Reservation, we continued our journey to Rapid City, South Dakota where, I purchased a book called *Bury My Heart at Wounded Knee* by Dee Brown. Over time this book would help cement my love for the Lakota people and their spiritual way of life. From Rapid City, we headed west into the Black Hills where, I felt a strange energy all around us most for of the time. It would be many years before I truly understood what this energy coming from the Black Hills was all about; more to come on that subject.

Shortly after we returned to San Antonio, a friend talked me into a business opportunity involving sales. Who would have believed a person who did not like people very much would take on a job in sales? You guessed it, Amway products. Go figure! I never would have believed I would have so much fun selling soap, but I did. It was not long before I began changing my opinion about people, especially people with upbeat personalities and Amway was full of them. What I learned from Amway was how to sell an idea as well as myself.

After four years in Amway, my interests moved toward scuba diving. Certified through Scuba Schools International (SSI) I became an advanced open water diver. Two years later, I attended the SSI Dive College to receive my advanced open water instructor's certificate. For the next five years, I instructed eight to ten students per class on how to dive safely in both fresh and salt water. What I learned from instructing scuba was how to teach and take responsibility for people's lives.

Today when I look back at the cookie crumbs of my life's experiences, it makes sense to me. I had to make some big changes in my negative thinking before I ever tried to help anyone with anything.

In February of 1989, an Apache/Hispanic friend named Kathy Stoops began pushing me to 'walk my talk'. The idea of picking up the pipe was beginning to have a draw for me, and so was the need to reach out to the Lakota for help. It took me fifteen years to make a lifetime commitment to carry the pipe and seek out the Lakota for guidance. Fifteen years is a drop in the bucket for spirits, as time for them is non-existent.

Chapter 2: First Pipe and Vision Quest

In this chapter I have written about events and visions of mine, because it gives me the opportunity to discuss what a vision is and how to interpret them.

In the early spring of 1989, my friend Kathy accompanied me on a trip to the Black Hills of South Dakota. There, she picked out a pipe crafted by a third-generation pipe maker named Swift Horse, and presented it to me. While visiting Prairie Edge, an American Indian art gallery in Rapid City, we met Charles Fast Horse an Oglala Lakota Medicine Man and artist reproducing Lakota weaponry and artifacts of the pre-reservation era. This meeting was not just coincidental; it set the stage for an enduring friendship that would change my life forever.

What I would learn that day was that the pipe is central to all ceremonies. One places seven pinches of a mixture called caŋśaśa (the inner bark of red willow) into the pipe bowl as prayers. When the pipe is smoked, the prayers float to the heavens via the smoke. Caŋśaśa is an herb; it is not tobacco or a drug. While looking through the Prairie Edge bookstore my friend found a book: *How to Take Part in Lakota Ceremonies*, by William Stolzman. As it turned out, this book was a great help in getting me moving on my spiritual quest. The real teachings would come from traditional Lakota over the many years yet to come.

Later that day we headed for a sacred place called Bear Butte, just northeast of the Black Hills, where I wanted to fill and smoke the pipe for the first time. We followed the winding path up the Butte to where we came to a small flat section a few feet off the path. Since we were the only people on the Butte, I was not worried about people walking up on me during our prayer time. My friend did not want to infringe on my time with the pipe so she decided to walk back down the Butte a little way off and pray in her own way.

After assembling the stone bowl (red pipe stone) to the pipe stem I began filling the pipe bowl with caŋśaśa to the seven directions, west, north, east, south, up, down and the center. (I will explain the reason for the seven directions in a later chapter.) Once filled, I lit a match and reached to hold it over the bowl of the pipe. Much to my surprise, I was unable to reach the bowl with the match due to the long length of the stem. I tried holding the pipe bowl above my head, to the left side, to the right side, between my knees, to no avail. Finally, I thought if I push the stem further into my mouth, I might be able to reach the bowl to light it. As I was pushing the stem further back into my mouth and trying to light the pipe, the stem hit my gag reflex almost causing me to lose my lunch.

As I sat there choking, I heard the most horrific sound coming from the area my friend was sitting in. Doubled up on the ground, she was laughing so hard she scarcely had time to breathe. She was not the only one laughing; I could hear the rocks, trees, and spirits of the Butte laughing as well. I was so glad I could brighten everyone's day, but I was determined to light this pipe. I picked up a stick, split the end, and inserted the end of a lit match. I held the end of the stick, easily reaching the bowl with the match and lit the pipe.

One lesson I took away was humility. I needed to slow down a little, as I needed to have the pipe awakened properly by a medicine man. This would be the last time I had trouble lighting the pipe. When people ask me, what changed, with a little grin, I hold both hands out in front of me, and say: 'My right arm became a little longer.' I believe it was more about relaxing and not taking myself so seriously.

Haŋbleceya

When we returned to San Antonio, Kathy helped me collect all the necessary items for my first haŋbleceya (crying for a vision, lamenting, or vision quest) to be held in an area called Chalk Bluff in southwestern Texas. I would have preferred someone like Fast Horse set up my first vision quest, but I felt a little odd in that I knew nothing about these ways and did not want to insult him with such a request. Driven by strong feelings, I took up the pipe to seek answers about who I was and what to do with the overwhelming feelings pushing me onto the 'good red road'. Therefore, I just went with the moment. Crazy as it sounds, I began preparing to put myself out on my first vision quest. I will not go into everything needed for a vision quest; it would take the better part of a chapter to explain. However, I will write a little about some of the items needed and what I experienced in the first 24 hours.

The haŋbleceya is one of the seven rites of the pipe. If you wish to get a better understanding of the seven rites, I suggest you read, *The Sacred Pipe- Black Elk's account of the seven rites of the Oglala Sioux*, by Joseph Epes Brown.

One of the first steps in preparing for your vision quest is the tobacco ties. A tobacco tie starts with a one-inch square piece of black cotton cloth. Add a prayer to a small pinch of tobacco and place it into the center of the cloth. Fold the cloth four times and tie it onto the end of a long string. Repeat this process until you add 100 black ties to the string spaced about one finger distance apart. The next color added to the string are 100 red ties, then 100 yellow ties, 100 white ties, 100 blue ties, and 100 green ties until 600 tobacco ties makes up a long string. By the time, you finish 600 tobacco ties, you've learned how to pray. If a Medicine Man is putting you up on the vision quest, you usually make 405 tobacco ties (for the 405 rock spirits of the Yuwipi man). The order of colors depends on the person putting you up on the haŋbleceya.

The next part of the prayer space is the flags: pieces of black cotton cloth three-inches wide by three-foot long. Place one large pinch of tobacco into one end of the flag as a prayer. Fold the end of the flag over four times and then tie to secure the ball of tobacco. Repeat this process until one black flag, one red flag, one yellow flag, one white flag, one blue flag, one red felt flag, and one green flag are prepared. Tie the flags onto seven straight fruit tree sticks about four feet long. (I will explain the reason for the colors in a later chapter.)

The vision quest site was in a heavily wooded area with a circular clearing at its center, about 40 feet in diameter. I flattened down the high grass in the area where I would be sitting. I then began to stick the seven flags into the ground. The black flag is in the northwest, the red flag in the northeast, the yellow flag in the southeast, and the white flag in the southwest. All the flags encompass approximately a 25-foot square area. One foot inside the white and black flags I set up the three remaining flags: blue, red felt, and green, from left to right, equally spaced.

Six inches inside the three flags, two forked sticks, 12 inches long, are stuck into the ground about 8 inches apart and a cross piece is used to connect them, like a drying rack. When one is not holding their pipe, it is set against this rack. Some people tie the pipe to their hand, and do not set it down the whole time they are on their vision quest.

The 600 tobacco ties wrap around the flags starting with the black flag in the northwest. I laid a blanket down to sit upon, filled my pipe, and began meditating to clear my mind.

As night time approached, I heard two birds moving through the tops of the trees. One bird 'meowed' like a cat, moving in a clockwise circle. The other made the sound of 'why,' moving in a counter clockwise circle. Throughout night they made these distinct sounds.

As the sun began to break through the darkness, I noticed thousands of Texas sized red ants surrounding the blanket I was sitting on. The sight of these monster-sized ants should have sent me running and I did think for just a moment, I should have sprayed the area, but my overall feeling was I would be all right. I noticed the ants were not coming onto the blanket, except for one confused ant that seemed to be lost. One thing I learned about the vision quest is nothing will cross the circle of ties to cause any harm. Therefore, with a little coaching with my finger, I directed the little fellow back into the grass. I noticed many ants were carrying grass cuttings back to their colony that just happened to be located inside the northwest perimeter of tobacco ties. They were not coming into my circle, they were already inside it.

Then I heard a voice say; *Watch the ants*. Therefore, I decided to pick out one of the ants to see what he was going to do. He took a hold of a piece of grass and began pulling it toward his colony opening. When he ran into an obstacle, he struggled until he overcame the obstacle and then continued his journey. This maneuvering continued many times until he hit the obstacle of obstacles. The little fellow was pulling and struggling with every fiber of his being but to no avail. I spoke out loud saying, "Why don't you just drop the grass and pick up the piece on the other side?" He continued struggling until a second ant passing by stopped, looked at him, and then took a hold of the other end of the grass, helping the first ant overcome the obstacle. When they had accomplished the feat together, the second ant moved on to collect his own burden. This struggle continued throughout the day with the entire ant colony working together to accomplish their tasks.

While studying these ants, I noticed a large deer tick crawling on my left arm. Remembering nothing will cross the circle of ties to cause any harm, I picked the tick off, threw it into the grass and continued watching the ants. Before long, I felt a tick crawling on my left arm again. This time I picked the tick off and said, 'Cut it out, or next time you will not be so lucky.' I was preparing to throw the pesky thing out of the circle when I heard the same voice say; *Watch the tick*. I threw the tick into the grass, but this time I noticed where it landed. That little dickens began running back towards where I sat and proceeded to climb back onto my left arm.

Once again, I removed the tick and tossed it into the grass. As sure as I was sitting on a blanket the same tick, commenced to run back with steadfast determination and climbed back onto my left arm. By this time, the vision quest was ending so, I picked everything up and bid farewell to my newly found friends. No, I did not keep the tick as a pet, but I did have a pet housefly once. That is a story for another chapter.

The two birds that kept me company the evening of my vision quest are symbolic in nature. The "meow" sound is a Catbird and the "why" sound must have been a spirit acting like the Heyóka, the contraries or clowns who do everything backwards. When a Catbird comes into your circle it suggests many people will be coming into your life. As of this writing, I have met thousands of people - most of whom have become my friends. The Heyóka moves in a counter- clockwise circle and are the most difficult to understand and work with. The meaning of 'why' was perceived by me as, 'Why are you here'? My answer was, 'I am supposed to be here.' As it turned out, I believe that was the correct answer to 'Why.' One of the lessons a person learns in the Lakota ways is, when a Heyóka says you are wrong, he is most likely saying you are right but then again, he may be saying you are wrong. Through their contrary statements and actions, the Heyóka challenges us to see if we truly believe in ourselves, as we walk along our spiritual path.

The red ants and tick were symbolic with respect to the vision. What I realized for myself from the red ants was I had a real problem working the obstacles in my life. When I ran into an obstacle, I would drop what I was doing and walk the other way, without confronting it. I was also terrible at asking for help in solving problems, or asking for directions. The red ants became one of my most powerful spiritual allies, as they helped me to take a real hard look at my behavior and slowly I began to make changes in my life. Today I have become much better at problem solving. If my wife is with me, I even stop to ask for directions, I am still working on that one.

The tick, I learned, is a member of the spider family, the Iktómi. The spider is considered the trickster. This little fellow showed me the way back to the Lakota. What I would learn when I first returned to the Lakota, was that they would ignore me or to put it another way, 'throw me away,' as if I were a pest. I would have to make many trips to the Lakota before they accepted me.

Over time, some of the Lakota took notice of me and only after gaining their trust would they begin the teachings. For over 200 years, the US Government and some mixed bloods made false statements and betrayed the Lakota with respect to the many treaties signed and then broken by the Government.

After the vision of the red ants, I can pray about it, leave some tobacco, and walk barefoot onto a large red ant colony. The reason for this is to collect the small stones the ants Carry to their entrance, as these stones are sacred, being they come from underground and are not contaminated. This is accomplished without their biting or upsetting the colony, and deer ticks no longer bit me. It had to do with a relationship established so long ago around the Lakota concept of Mitakúye Oyasin (We Are All Related.) Both the red ants and the ticks became my spiritual allies.

Chapter 3: Lakota Traditions and Beliefs

Before we get into Black Elk's vision, I would like to share some of the more important traditions and beliefs of the Lakota.

Fast Horse once told me, "Quentin, all you have to do is show up and be real; the spirits already know who you are." With this in mind, if you are anything but "real" in your pursuit of spirituality and the spirits bring you a vision, they may have to get creative. If you are not in-balance and focused, you may not realize the vision given to you even if the spirits handed it to you in a book.

When a traditional Lakota person (one that follows the Lakota spiritual way of life) goes on a hunt, picks up stones, sage or red willow, etc. They ask permission in prayer and then leave tobacco as an offering of appreciation; these things are not ours to take. It is important to understand the term Mitakúye Oyasin, one of the more important statements in the Lakota language that means, 'We Are All Related.' Mitakúye Oyasin is not just another statement; it is a state of being, not above or below but a relationship with all things.

A vision consists of the spiritual world encountering the natural world, for example, a small bird talking. Traditional Lakota commonly understand these events. When a traditional Lakota person has a vision, it takes seat on their soul like the hard drive in a computer. When they think of the vision, it plays back as if it had just happened. They do not add or take anything away from the original vision regardless of how much time has elapsed; it lives within them. This is a way of Lakota life. The Lakota perfected the art of the oral tradition of storytelling. The beauty of this type of communication is that the story does not lose its meaning due to changes in the spoken word like that of the written word.

A Lakota elder once said, "In some circles they would medicate me for stating I see spirits, hear voices, and talk with spirits." He went on to say, "In some cases, people diagnosed with schizophrenia might not be sick at all. There are two types of spirits: Positives and Negatives. When a Positive spirit interacts with you, they give you just enough information to get you moving, then step back to see what you will do with it, like a good parent. The Negative spirit will overload you with information, trying to control you. In some cases, could this perhaps be schizophrenia?" It is important to understand that traditional Indian people know the difference between Positive and Negative spirits. They do not let them run their lives. They take what information they need and leave the rest. It is called being in spiritual balance.

Chapter 4: Early Boyhood

The following is a summary account from John G. Neihardt's *Black Elk Speaks*, Chapter 2 Early Boyhood.

Black Elk:

Black Elk said he was born in the December Moon, when the trees were popping, and when the four Crows (Indians) were killed, 1863.

He went on to say he was three years old when his father broke his right leg during the fight of the Hundred Slain.

Clarification:

The Lakota, like many tribes, used the cycles of the Moon and current events to establish the month and time of year. The 'Moon of trees popping' represents the crackling sound the cottonwood trees make when they began to freeze in December. The date of Black Elk's birth is established when the four Crows (Indians) were killed. In ancient times, before the coming of the Europeans to North America, the Indian used 13 moons to represent one year. With the advent of the modern calendar, they dropped one moon from the middle of the year, and began working with 12 moons.

The fight of the Hundred Slain was the Fetterman Fight of 1866 when the Lakota killed over 80 soldiers on Peno Creek and where Black Elk's father broke his leg. This established Black Elk's third birthday. Chosen Lakota would keep a winter count on tanned hides. They did not have a written language, so they drew sketches of people, places, and things in a clockwise circular pattern, depicting events for each moon to mark a period in time.

Black Elk:

He said he was five years old when his Grandfather made him a bow and arrows. He was out riding on horseback when a thunderstorm was coming from the west. He looked and saw a Kingbird sitting in a tree, and was going to shoot the bird when the bird spoke and said; *The clouds are one-sided; the voice is calling!* He noticed two men flying from the clouds, headfirst as they come down, singing a song as they made thunder.

They came from the north, where the white giant lives. When they were close, they turned toward the west, became geese, and disappeared. He never spoke of this vision with anyone. It was fun to think about, but he was too afraid to share it.

Clarification:

Can you imagine sending a five-year-old out riding a horse and hunting with a bow? Within Chapter 3 of *Black Elk Speaks*, Black Elk explains: "Lakota boys learn the ways of a warrior by just watching, and practiced what they saw." He said, "We were warriors when we were 14 years old."

When the Kingbird spoke to Black Elk, it stated; *The clouds are one-sided.* First, the clouds were that of a thunderstorm the Wakíyaŋ Oýate (Thunder Being People). To speak the truth is important to the Lakota; a person who lies has a forked tongue. A two-faced person cannot be trusted. The clouds are one-sided, not two-faced, something Black Elk could trust in.

The Dr. James (Jim) E. Gillihan Connection

In 1972 Dr. James (Jim) E. Gillihan (1935-2002) a Cherokee elder became the director of the National History Museum of the University of South Dakota. He would visit the elders as part of his work and became good friends with Frank Fools Crow, the spiritual leader and medicine man of the Lakota Nation. Dr. Gillihan also became friends with other religious leaders such as Lame Deer, Henry Crow Dog, Matthew King, and Joe Rock Boy. They taught him their language, traditions, and ceremonies within the Lakota/Dakota spiritual way of life. Rock Boy adopted Dr. Gillihan in the way of the Lakota, and gave him the name Tatanka Ska (White Buffalo). All these men wished to share an earth-centered way of life with all people regardless of their race, color, sex, or religious views. They taught Dr. Gillihan to do the same.

In 1991, Dr. Gillihan became one of my friends and teachers. Over the years, he shared many teachings with me; one of the teachings was how the soul enters a baby at birth. He went on to say, when the Lakota midwives were helping to deliver a baby they did not allow dogs to be in the room. The women kept their mouths closed because when the baby opened its mouth to take its first breath, the soul would enter through the mouth of the child dividing into four parts. One part attaches to the placenta, Cekṗa (twin) the connection with nature. The family placed a part of the umbilical cord into a turtle amulet for a girl and a lizard amulet for a boy. These talismans stayed with the child throughout their lives to keep them safe from harm. One part becomes the aura or shadow, Naġí (the Guardian). One part resides at the top of the head, To'wakaŋ (the Advanced Guardian). One part takes seat at the solar plexus just below the heart, Niya' (the Breath of Life, heart/mind/lungs).

He went on to explain how the Cekṗa is placed into the crook of a tree and whichever animal ate it became the child's ally for life, for it now shares a part of their soul. The soul part of the aura, the Naġí, would know everything that is happening around you, the 'gut' feeling. If there was danger, it would report to you, for example, 'Do not go there', or 'something is wrong;' it is our intuition. A Wanáġi, is a ghost. The soul part on the top of the head, the To'wakaŋ, could travel to an area you were planning to visit and report back as to whether everything is okay or not: "again our intuition." It even can travel into your future and report back, déjàvu or 'the sense of': I have been here before, when you know you have not. The part of the soul that takes seat at the solar plexus, the Niya' just below the heart impeccably runs the entire body chemistry; I have also heard this referred to as the subconscious.

Now back to the Kingbirds' conversation. I think we can agree King-birds, eagles, horses, and the like would not speak the Lakota language or even English. They all have their own language, and Kingbirds do quite well in communicating with each other. Then, how do you suppose Black Elk heard the Kingbird say; *The clouds are one-sided; the voice is calling.* If the spirits need to use a Kingbird to get the message to us, they most certainly will. The time to pay attention is when an animal is acting out in a manner not normal to their behavior. The voice would have been that of a spirit, heard by the Niya' not the ear. The voice could also have been that of the Naǧi or the To'wakaŋ, when I look back on my experience, it all adds up.

Black Elk had indicated he was afraid to speak of the Kingbird or the two Wakíyaŋ (Thunder Beings) he had encountered. In the Lakota, spiritual way of life, to become a warrior, a young man petitions with a pipe, asking a Medicine Man or elder to put him on a hill where he would seek or cry for his vision. If they smoked his pipe, it meant they would honor his request. Some people spend years seeking their vision, going on a hill each year to pray, four days and four nights, without receiving their vision. Black Elk was not looking for a vision at five years of age. He was just being a boy, and the spirits came to him. One could understand why he felt a little intimidated.

A Time to Reflect

The following is an account of my first contact with the voice, and the Lakota spiritual way of life:

It was the summer of 1950, when I was six years old. My mother and father had divorced a year earlier. My older brother, Stephan, moved with my father to Reno, Nevada. I stayed with my mother and older sister, Kathy Watson, living in Corte Madera, California, a small town just north of San Francisco.

My mother was in a relationship with a man named Mike, who moved in with us, along with an enormous Great Dane. The problem for me was this dog hated little children, and Mike and my mother both were alcoholics spending most evenings hanging out at a tavern.

Kathy, a 13-year-old who did not want to be bothered with a little 6-year-old brother, was okay with my spending the evenings out on the front porch. For me, the porch was a safer place to be than inside the house with a vicious dog that hated children. I was literally afraid of everything: the dark, the huge redwood forest with all its animals, my sister, the dog, Mike, and my own shadow.

One evening, Kathy came up with a solution, which she thought would work for both of us. She said, "If you will run to the store and get me a package of Hostess cupcakes and a Coke, I will let you into your bedroom, away from the dog." The main concern for me was it was always after 9 pm, dark, and I had to walk down the middle of the road, for I was sure monsters were waiting for me from both sides of the road.

The other choice was a shortcut through the forest, along a narrow path. On one of those evenings, I elected to take the shortcut. As I was hurrying along, I came across something sitting in the middle of the path. As I drew closer, I noticed it was a large wolf, just sitting there looking at me. My head said run, but my feet were not getting the message. I just stood there paralyzed; it felt like my hair was standing on end, with my mouth and eyes wide open. I could not even scream.

Unexpectedly, I heard a voice say; *Why are you afraid of the forest?* My first thought was someone was standing next to this wolf, only to realize there was no one there. Then the voice said; *The forest is like your mother, and these animals are like your family; you have nothing to fear tonight.* The wolf stood up, turned to the left, and trotted off into the woods, looking over its shoulder at me as if it were smiling, and then disappeared into the darkness.

Calmness came over me and surprisingly, I was no longer afraid. Slowly, I proceeded to walk through the forest, listening to all the sounds of wildlife coming from it. When I arrived at the store, I purchased one Coke and one package of Hostess cupcakes. For those of you who are not familiar with how they packaged cupcakes in the 50's, it consisted of a light cardboard bottom with a covering of clear cellophane.

Here is where the tables began to turn; I opened one end of the cellophane exposing the bottom of one cupcake. You guessed it; I inserted one of my tiny little fingers, extracting all the whipped cream out of the cupcake. I sealed the hole up and proceeded to work from the other end on the next cupcake. When I had my fill of whipped cream, I sealed up the wrapper and delivered the hollow remains to 'sister ugly', a name I kept to myself, of course. From that day on, she thought Hostess stopped putting whipped cream in their cupcakes, and to this day, I have not told her what I did. If she ever reads this book, I hope she does not gag, thinking about my dirty little fingers poking around inside her cupcakes.

About a year later, my mother sent me to live with my father, his new wife, Eleanor, her daughter, Dale, and my brother, Stephan. What a real plus. I had a new family: a father, mother, brother, and now a younger sister, at least until I was fourteen, and then had to move back with my mother. She had been sober for seven years, and until her death in 2004, she did not touch alcohol again. For the next forty-six years, we would have a mother-son relationship.

As a young boy, I never spoke with anyone about the wolf in the woods, partly because I did not want people to think I was strange or try to talk me out of what I knew to be real. When a child speaks of invisible friends, often society passes it off as make-believe. That night in the woods so long ago was anything but make-believe.

At the time, I had no idea what was happening, I just knew whatever that was, saved me from a life of fear. What I have learned about the wolf is they represent family, helping each other through all aspects of life, something I was lacking in my own family at that time.

I will never forget that evening in 1950, when spirit let me know that I was not alone.

Chapter 5: Coyote and the Crows

The following events are experiences Black Elk and I had involving crows and a coyote and how they interacted with us. The reason I chose to write about these events is to shed some light on how spirits use the two-legged, four-legged, and winged to get our attention.

Take Care, Old Friend

On December of 1987, my two-year-old daughter, Samantha, her mother, Jane, and I were visiting with Samantha's grandmother, Maria, and grandfather, John, in Pueblo, Colorado. John was experiencing some minor abdominal problems and was admitted to the hospital for observation. It was our intention to spend a few days with John and Maria before heading to the mountains for some downhill skiing.

Maria and Jane made plans to visit John in the hospital that afternoon while I stayed with Samantha, as she was too young to visit. It was one of those warm December days as Samantha played with the dog in the yard, and I sat in a lawn chair looking out at the snow-capped mountains in the west when, I noticed a black dot against the mountains that seemed to be moving towards us. As it drew closer, I recognized it to be a large crow, which made one tight clockwise circle around Maria's home at about twenty feet off the ground. It looked down at us and began making a loud cawing sound as it finished circling and then headed back in the direction from whence it came, disappearing into the snow-capped mountains.

A strange feeling came over me as I watched the crow disappear into the mountains. Later that day, Maria and Jane returned to the house with good news about John. They said he was doing much better and his

Doctor had cleared his immediate health problem. Maria said I could stop by in the morning to visit with him while they kept an eye on Samantha. I did not want to say anything to Maria to upset her, so I spoke with Jane privately that evening. I told her about the crow and how it had acted, and felt that John would not make it through the night.

She insisted John was doing better and he was looking forward to seeing me in the morning. At 3:00 am, the call came. John had made his spirit journey. Jane never looked at me the same way after that, she would always say, "You and your Indian stuff." All I know is, John was an old friend, and his spirit found a way to say goodbye through the crow's message. This was my first encounter with a crow; it would not be the last.

The following is a summary account from John G. Neihardt's Black *Elk Speaks*, Chapter 12 Grandmother's Land.

Black Elk:
Black Elk was lying in a buffalo robe when he heard a coyote howl. He seemed to understand what it was saying; *On the ridge, west of here, there are buffalo, but first you will see two more people not too far off.*

He woke his Father and told him what the coyote had said. His father had been noticing Black Elk's power and believed him. The next morning just before they came to the ridge, they saw two horses, huddled in the brush. They noticed a shelter made from a buffalo robe in the brush. In there they encountered an old Lakota man and a boy. The four climbed the ridge and waited. Soon they saw the head of a bull buffalo coming past them below the hill. Then seven more buffalo appeared, the two old men shot first and killed one and the boys killed seven buffalo.

Clarification:

Spirit spoke with Black Elk's Guardian (the Naĝí) telling him of the two Lakota and the buffalo on the ridge, a time when Black Elk and his father desperately needed their help.

The following is a summary account from John G. Neihardt's *Black Elk Speaks*, Chapter 13, The Compelling Fear

Black Elk:

Black Elk and a small party of his people wanted to leave Canada and return to their homeland in the Dakotas. They set out with only a small number of horses as many had died from the hard winter. After a long day, they camped along the All-Gone-tree Creek. Black Elk decided to take the horses out to feed on the tender grass, when a strange feeling came over him. He heard a voice say; *Watch! You will see something!* He climbed to where some large rocks were scattered, and laid down beside them looking around. He saw two Blackfeet warriors (not the Sihasapa Lakota) crawling up on the opposite hill, a stone throw away. At the top of the hill, they peered over into the Lakota camp. Black Elk heard them talking and knew they were planning an attack on his small village. After they left, he returned to his village and warned his people of the pending attack.

They did not even wait to break down their tepees and just left them standing. They traveled fast into the night to escape their enemy, and crossed a fast-moving creek almost losing the old women. As they traveled, sounds of gun shots erupted back at their abandoned camp. It was growing darker; a thunderstorm came and stayed with them throughout the night to protect them until morning, but hardly any rain fell upon them throughout the night.

Clarification:

Black Elk's Nagî was hearing spirit; *Watch! You will see something!* Had he not listened; his small band would have been lost to the warriors.

You Can Go Back Now

In the fall of 1994, I met a man named Steve No Hands, a Cherokee elder. His heart was only functioning at twenty-five percent, so he asked one of his friends to escort me to the hospital to visit with him. I was not a medicine man but knew how to pray with the pipe so, I agreed to meet with him. He said, "I do not want to die a white man." He went on to say that if the Great Spirit would allow me to live a little longer, I would dedicate the rest of my life toward learning the American Indian's spiritual way of life. Steve's friends and I filled the pipe in his room, putting in prayers for his recovery, and then took the pipe outdoors to smoke. One week later Steve came home from the hospital and joined our little family to begin his quest for knowledge.

Five years later, in the summer of 1999, Steve petitioned me with tobacco and asked if I would watch over his soul if he were to pass over before learning more about this spiritual way of life. One month later, my old friend passed into the spirit world. His wife who respected his wish assembled the necessary items, presented me with the bundle, and petitioned me to hold it for one year. Holding a bundle can be difficult, as it changes the way one interacts with others. A person holding a bundle cannot argue or fight with people, use a weapon, or even a steak knife. You either eat with your fingers or get someone else to cut up your food.

For the next twelve months, I worked extremely hard to keep all negative energy away from the bundle. One of the more difficult challenges for me in the last five months was dealing with some petty discord within our

Tióśpaye (extended family.) There were five or six out of a group of sixty people creating a real hardship with respect to my then fiancée, Ginger. Judgements like, "Who does Ginger think she is, the first lady." To put it in simple terms, it was just petty jealousy toward Ginger; one of the many tools of negative force. I was unable to resolve this problem at the time, as the bundle was too important to engage in this negative pettiness.

At the end of the year, one week before the releasing ceremony was to take place, I made what was to be an eight-mile walk down an old mule towpath running parallel to the Illinois River. After walking approximately two miles, I came across some cattails growing alongside the river channel. Attached to the cattails was a large spider web, about 18 inches in diameter. The morning dew had settled onto the web sparkling like small diamonds in the sunlight. At its center sat a red and yellow Iktómi (spider) about one and one half inches in diameter. I stood there staring at this spectacular piece of work when a voice said; *You can go back now.* I had two miles yet to go before turning around to complete an eight-mile walk. However, for some reason they (spirits) wanted me to go back after only completing two miles.

As I turned and began walking back, I was thinking that four miles would just have to do. About five minutes had passed when I heard the most horrible screeching coming toward me from the channel. I looked up to see a crow flying fast and erratically with a Cooper Hawk hot on his tail feathers. When they reached the point where I was standing, the crow made a hard-right flying to the opposite side of the channel, and landed in a tree. The hawk made one circle around the crow and then landed in a tree about ten feet away from the crow. At this point, the crow was terribly upset and began cawing loudly when just then, two more crows flew in.

The three crows sat together scolding the little hawk who just sat across from them looking rather plucky. After a minute or so of the crows hollering, the little Cooper Hawk leaped out of the tree and flew straight at the crows. He made one tight circle around all three of them and then flew back to the tree where he was perched. The crows looked a little confused, muttered a bit, and then the two that came to the rescue turned and flew off, leaving the first crow to his demise. The little hawk jumped from his perch and sailed back up the channel from whence he had come.

As I watched the hawk disappear through the trees, a voice said; *Sometimes, you must stand up for who you are.* I thought about what I had just witnessed and decided after the soul releasing, I would address the group that was creating hardship for Ginger and me. As for the crows and hawk, it is most always the crows chasing and harassing hawks. On this day, the hawk stood up for who it was and the crows took notice.

One week later, with the help of over sixty people and Dr. Gillihan, we set up the soul releasing for Steve No Hands to help him on his spirit journey. The keeping and releasing of the soul ceremony is one of the seven rites of the pipe. Dr. Gillihan said Fools Crow had shown him the simple version of the keeping and releasing of the soul ceremony when a Medicine Man is not available, so that is the method we used.

After the releasing ceremony was complete, I took the opportunity to speak to the entire group that evening. Without naming names, I admonished those who were so cruel towards Ginger, stating she sat at my right and I did not appreciate their taking advantage of the fact that I was keeping a bundle during the months of their petty attacks toward her. I went on to say, the way I was taught, men do not give teachings to women with respect to women's issues. This is the main reason Ginger is involved with the new women coming into our circle.

Sometimes, you must stand up for who you are.

Stay Alert

It was after 10:00 pm on Thursday, July 1992. While watching the last ten minutes of the evening news I noticed tiny discs of blue, red, and white lights darting in and around my pipe bundle. After a few minutes, the discs of light slowly vanished and the room became calm again. I must have been incredibly tired that evening, as I do not remember my head hitting the pillow. At 4:00 am, something woke me. I looked through the open door and noticed colorful little lights darting around the living room. Feeling odd, I smudged the room with sage and decided to fill the pipe and pray about what I was witnessing. When I finished smoking the pipe, I heard a voice say; *Stay alert, something is going to happen!*

For the remainder of the day, I was involved in designing a new product. I became so immersed in my work, I had forgotten all about the pipe, and the warning to stay alert. I shared an office with a fellow engineer by the name of Sandy. Her son, Don, was taking his morning break in our office, when a crow landed on the roof's gutter system and began cawing loudly. I began to experience the same odd feeling I had Thursday evening, so I walked over to the window and looked up, attempting to see what this loud cawing was all about. Due to the roof overhang, I was unable to see the crow but it was certainly making its presence known. As Don was leaving the office, he looked over at me in a perplexed way and then exited the room. At that moment, the crow departed, cawing loudly as he flew.

About thirty minutes had passed when Sandy returned to the office. She said, "My son was telling me about the crow thing, what is that all about?" Her question was like a trigger, starting a download of information. I seemed to know precisely what the little lights and the crow meant. I told Sandy I thought there was a message for both Don and myself with respect to our cars. We both need to be careful about the next day or two and pay close attention to our driving.

Looking at me in a strange manner, Sandy asked if crows were messengers of doom. I said, "Not normally, most crows are just being crows, but every now and then spirits will use anything to get our attention, which could include a crow." I told her it would not hurt to let her son know about driving with care. In fact, she should pay attention to her own driving, as well.

It was about 3:20 pm when a voice said; *Sandy did not tell Don to drive with care and he is getting ready to leave for home.*

My thoughts were, 'So what? I am not going to tell some kid that a crow told me about his driving problems.'

The voice said; *He is washing his hands in the bathroom and he would be alone.*

I walked out of the office muttering, 'He had better be alone, only to find him where 'they' (The voice) said he would be. I asked Don if his mother had spoken with him about the crow. Don just looked at me in weird sort of way and said, "No."

Against my better judgment, I repeated what I had told his mother earlier and suggested he take extra care when driving for the next couple of days. Don began laughing as he threw the paper towel in the trash and walked out of the room. My first thought was, 'they' set me up good this time, but then remembered not everyone moves with spirit. I did what 'they' asked of me and that would have to suffice. At this point, it would be up to me to follow my own vision and stay alert.

As I prepared to leave the office that evening, the thought of the crow began to gnaw at me. What did this entire thing mean and why did they include Don in this? I was not going to take any chances with its meaning, so I was vigilant when driving the short distance home. Later that evening, I decided to pick up a few items from the store and headed out again, the whole time thinking of the warning, stay alert, something is going to happen!

I had traveled about one mile on a two-lane road when I noticed a young 13 or 14-year-old boy coming toward me on his bicycle. He was riding against traffic, about 200 feet from me when the voice said; *Get ready.* I covered the brake with my left foot when the front tire of the bicycle abruptly hit a pothole, throwing the boy from the bike into the middle of my lane. I immediately hit the brakes and stopped within a few feet of him. Realizing his predicament, the youngster scrambled to the edge of the road, where he sat picking gravel out of his hands.

I asked him if he was all right, he said he was and thanked me for not running over him, jumped back onto his bicycle, and continued his journey. I thought to myself, if I had been going any faster or had not been paying as close attention to my driving, I do not believe I would have been able to stop in time.

When I arrived at work Monday morning and noticed Don was not taking his morning break in our office, I asked his mother how he was doing. She said, "He was backing out of the driveway Saturday morning and ran into his sister's car causing over $2,500 in damages to her car."

I thought to myself, 'I guess you could say the crow was two for two that weekend,' and no, I did not say, 'I told you so.' The To'wakaŋ and the Naġi were the two soul connections reporting back to me stating; *Stay alert, something is going to happen. Get ready.*

I believe spirit was teaching me how to pay attention to my guardians, the To'wakaŋ and the Naġi. Don's misfortune with his sister's car and the young boy on the bike, turned out to be eye openers for me.

Chapter 6: The Bay Horse

The following is a summary account from John G. Neihardt's *Black Elk Speaks*, Chapter 3 The Great Vision,

Black Elk:

At the beginning of Chapter 3 of the Great Vision, Black Elk recalls the summer when he was nine-years old (1872) and the people were content during the winters and summers even though the wasichu made their iron road (railroad) alongside the Platte River dividing the buffalo heard in half.

Clarification:

Originally the term wasichu referred to the coming of the Europeans to North America - non-Indian people. Over time, its meaning would change to refer to, people without number (more than can be counted), or more than the stars in the night sky. I have heard the term used, so many people you cannot get rid of them. When the Lakota began to have more contact with the US Government around 1850, the word wasichu took on a darker meaning: 'fat takers'. The term 'fat takers' represents the non-Indian and US Government's behavior in that they take the best parts of everything and left the Lakota with the scraps.

Black Elk:

Black Elk recalls hearing voices from the time he was five-years old, until the summer when he was nine-years old. He had no idea what they needed from him and when he did not hear the voices, he just put them behind him; he was a young boy hunting and riding horses.

Clarification:

The description of the soul connection Niya', in Chapter 2, should explain why Black Elk was hearing voices from the time he was five through to the time when summer approached and he was nine years old. The spirits were simply teaching him to listen, until it was time for him to meet with them. Sometimes I hear voices with my ears but most of the time, I hear voices with my Niya', Naġi, or To'wakaŋ - clear deep profound thoughts coming out of nowhere.

Black Elk:

During the summer when Black Elk was nine years old, he and his people headed northwest into Montana. They made camp alongside a small creek not far from the Greasy Grass. A friend named Man Hip invited Black Elk to join him for supper in his lodge.

During the visit, Black Elk heard a voice say; *The spirits have sent for you, come.* He believed the voice to be real, so he got up and went outside the lodge. When he was outside, both his legs began hurting, and then the voice just faded away, leaving him alone. When he returned, Man Hip asked if everything was all right, Black Elk said his legs are sore.

Clarification:

Black Elk heard the voice loud and clear and the fact that Man Hip did not hear the voice suggests it must have been Black Elk's To'wakaŋ hearing the voice. And the fact that Black Elk's legs were hurting him suggests the spirits did not want the physical boy to come with them. It would be Black Elk's To'wakaŋ which would make this journey; an out of body experience.

Black Elk:

The following morning Black Elk was out riding with his friends. When they dismounted to get some water from a creek, Black Elk's legs gave out. His friends helped him up onto his horse and by the end of the day, he was dreadfully sick. By the next day Black Elk's arms and legs were badly inflamed.

As Black Elk lay resting in his lodge, he peered through the opening and saw the same two men who had come to him when he was five-years old, flying from the clouds, headfirst as they came down. Sharp Lightning flashed from their spears as they came. When they were on the ground they said; *Make haste, the Grandfathers request your presence.* Then they turned and flew upward to return to the clouds from whence they came.

As Black Elk stood to follow the two men he noticed that his legs no longer hurt him. He said, a little cloud came from where the two men were flying, stopped, picked him up, and followed the two men flying.

Clarification:

The one thing I have learned about the To'wakaŋ is, when it is working, you had better be sitting extremely still. If the Six Grandfathers (the term Grandfather is used to show respect) were going to spend twelve days with Black Elk's To'wakaŋ, they would make sure his physical body stayed put and that is precisely what they did. The two men flying headfirst were thunder beings, his escorts. The fact that Black Elk's legs did not hurt him and he was so light he could ride on the little cloud, confirms that it was his To'wakaŋ making this great journey.

Many students have asked me why Black Elk received such a powerful vision at nine years old. At nine, Black Elk had a pure soul; he was not a warrior nor had he learned the ways of men. If one thinks about it, some people send their children to Sunday school or church camp to learn from trusted people about God. I guess you could say Black Elk received teachings from the best of them: a twelve-day church camp surrounded by images of things a young Lakota boy could understand. The other reason is a traditional Lakota person listens to spirits and then attempts to live within its teachings. I believe, the most important reason for spirits placing such an important vision with Black Elk is, he would not try to change his vision, or control those who attempt to live by it. This is a Lakota way of life, one does not add or take anything away from their vision.

Earlier in the book, I stated some visions take a lifetime to realize. What the Six Grandfathers taught Black Elk would live within his soul for the rest of his life. The parts of this vision that he did not understand at nine would become clearer with time and within events throughout his life.

In Chapter 1, I did not reveal the identity of the two spirits that visited me during my meditation in the summer of 1973. One of them was my spirit ally; some would refer to this spirit as my guardian angel. This was the first time I had seen him. To this day, I am unable to describe what he looks like. The other spirit was my To'wakaŋ and he looked just like me. It was like looking into a mirror.

Black Elk:

Soon Black Elk found himself and the two men amidst a world of clouds with hills and mountains; it was silent but he could hear a slight murmur

The two men said; *Observe the four-legged one!* Black Elk noticed a bay horse looking at them and then the horse said; *Pay attention to me! My life's story you shall observe.*

Clarification:

The great white plain with snowy hills and mountains is representative of the spirit world. As I was taught, the spirit world is a mirror of the natural world, the place where we exist. In a later chapter, I will spend considerable time going over this concept. The two thunder beings introduced Black Elk to his main spirit ally, the bay horse. The horse was an important ally to the Lakota; it was like a member of their family. Before the horse, the dogs would help carry their belongings, tipi (or tepee), clothing, cooking utensils, etc. They hunted on foot, limiting the amount of game they could carry. With the coming of the horse, the tepee became larger and they could hunt buffalo on horseback more efficiently. To the Lakota, the horse represented power, speed and freedom.

Remember the Kingbird, ants, and ticks, a spirit can take any shape it needs to get your attention. The color of the bay horse is important, as it represents both purity and power. A reddish-brown body with a black mane, tail, ears, and lower legs characterizes the bay horse. Red represents purity and endurance, the traditional color of the north. Black represents the power of the west, the thunder beings.

Black Elk:

The bay horse turned toward the west and said; *Pay attention to them! Their life's story you shall realize.* Black Elk noticed a dozen black horses standing side by side wearing a string of buffalo hooves around their necks. The sight of them was striking but he was afraid as lightning flashed from their manes with thunder coming from their nostrils.

Clarification:

The number twelve is a sacred number, it can represent one complete year. Twelve can also be divided by the sacred number four, four seasons, four directions. The twelve black horses represent the color of the west where the thunder being people live. The string of buffalo hooves represents the thundering sound the hooves make as the buffalo runs across the Plains. The Lakota had a use for all parts of the buffalo: food, clothing, shelter, tools, and from the hooves, glue.

Thunder beings can take many forms: men, horses, eagles, etc. When the thunder beings come from the west they bring fear and destruction. After they pass over the earth, all its inhabitants come to life. For without the thunder beings, life as we know it would not exist.

An elder and I spoke about why the thunder beings create so much destruction. He said, "They are making way for new life to exist. They do not intentionally cause death or destruction, they do not mean to cause harm, it is just what they are."

Another function of the thunder beings is to guard the Inipi (sweat lodge) against abuse by people who do not understand the age-old traditions and any negative spirits that would try to enter the lodge uninvited.

When a person has a vision of thunder beings, they could become a Heyóka; they could even possess the power to influence the weather. With this power comes a price, a true Heyóka has trouble holding down a job or communicating with people, as everything they say and do can come out backwards or contrary. Being a true Heyóka is a 24/7 thing, not just on weekends or ceremonial days, they are always in service to the people and spirit. My experience is that the true Heyóka is a rarity, few in number. As we get deeper into Black Elk's vision, I will explain how this played out for him. The vision of the Kingbird and the two thunder beings were just precursors of much bigger things to come for him.

Black Elk:

Turning toward the north, the place of the great white giant, the bay horse said; *Pay attention!* Black Elk noticed a dozen white horses standing side by side their manes were like the mighty wind of a snowstorm, and from their nostrils a deafening sound, with white geese circling all around the horses.

Clarification:

Fast Horse said, "In the north, the great white giant covers the earth with its wing, creating snow, separating the good seeds from the bad seeds, the vitalizer."

The twelve white horses represent the color of that direction and the white geese represent the power of a snowstorm as they launch into the sky sending their sacred voices and filling the sky with white wings. They also represent endurance, courage, and bravery. An elder once told me that

46

people should not whine as much about the cold winters. He said, "Get off your couch and shovel some snow, it will build endurance, strength and improve the immune system."

Black Elk:

Turning toward the east, the place where the sun shines constantly, the bay horse said; *Pay attention!* Black Elk noticed a dozen sorrel horses standing side by side wearing ribbons of elk teeth. Their manes were like sunrise light, with eyes glowing like the morning star.

Clarification:

The east is where the morning star (Venus) lives; it appears in the east just before sunrise and brings us knowledge and wisdom. The twelve sorrel horses (reddish) represent the color of that direction and the morning star. The necklaces of elk's teeth have a spiritual significance for the Lakota. When a boy was born, he might receive an elk tooth, as it represented a long life; the tooth was the last part of the elk to return to the earth after death. When a young Lakota warrior dreamed of an elk, he believed he would have courage, strength, and sexual superiority over other men.

Black Elk:

Turning toward the south, the place where all things face, the bay horse said; *Pay attention!* Black Elk noticed a dozen buckskin horses, standing side by side with antlers growing on their heads and manes alive like trees and grasses.

Clarification:

The twelve buckskin horses (yellowish) represent the color of the southern direction, the power to grow (spring). As I was taught, the statement, 'where all things face,' represents the walk of the 'good red road'. When we travel on the 'good red road' we are moving from north to south thus, we are always facing the south. It is also the place our deceased spirit begins its journey up and along the Milky Way. The north is where souls of our deceased relatives wait until it is time to enter the open mouth of a newborn. It can also mean, we are born in the south (infancy), and move to the west (youth, where we find our power). Then we move to the north (middle age, where we find our gray hair), then to the east (old age, where we find wisdom and knowledge) and return to the south as we prepare to make our spirit journey: the four divides of life.

The 'good red road' is a spiritual reference to the four directions. From the north through to the south is the 'good red road', the spiritual road. An elder once told me, the negative force lies on the left side of the 'red road'; the positive force is located on the right side. When we walk the 'red road', we move into the left, the negative side, and then cross back onto the 'red road'. We continue down the 'red road' and then move into the right, the positive side and then cross back onto the 'red road'.

One repeats this process throughout their life taking a little from both. In doing this, we experience both positive and negative forces. If we were to walk the 'good red road' straight through without moving through positive and negative forces, we would learn little about positive and negative emotions. What is important to remember is we need to cross back onto the 'red road' each time. To do so is called being in spiritual balance.

If a person chose to stay on the negative side of the 'red road', and does not cross back, then fear might consume them. Fear is the root of all negative emotions such as anger, hate, jealousy (resentment), and greed to name a few. If a person chose to stay on the positive side of the 'red road', and does not cross back, then courage might consume them. Courage is the root of all positive emotions such as calm, love, admiration, and charity, to name a few.

The real problem with being in a spiritual low or high is we are unable to contribute to the natural world. We cannot maintain a state of balance in the spiritual world in either the negative or positive; over time sickness and death will follow. An example of how one works with negative and positive emotions can be explained this way. You are standing on some railroad tracks and a train is approaching, what gets you off the tracks? Certainly, it would not be courage, then how about fear? Fear can be a great motivator to cause you to jump out of the way of the train. What is important to understand is after the train has passed, you must put the fear away. If you hold onto fear, you will be afraid of trains for the rest of your life. If we think of these emotions as tools of negative or positive force then, a person can simply look at borrowing them for a short time and then putting them back when we are finished using them.

Let me make myself clear here, causing harm to people, places, or things does not constitute simple borrowing of negative force. What we put into life, is what we get back.

Black Elk:

The bay horse said; *Your Grandfathers require your presence, the four-horse troupe will escort you, be brave.* Black Elk watched as all the horses fell into lines of four, side by side. First the twelve black horses, then the twelve white, the twelve sorrel and the twelve buckskins horses, all marching four by four behind the bay. Turning to the west the bay whinnied and the sky filled with horses of all colors making the sound of thunder, leaping and diving. The bay then turned to the north whinnied and the sky was filled with leaping and diving horses of every color, like a blizzard wind. To the east, he whinnied and horses reported in every color with manes and tails bright as sunlight whinnying back. Finally, the bay called to the south and horses of every color diving, twisting and joyfully whinnying back.

Clarification:

What the bay horse was showing Black Elk was that from the west the horses were like a thunderstorm, with every color. From the north came horses like a snowstorm, with every color. From the east, horses with glowing manes and tails like the morning light with every color; and from the south, horses of every color happy, like springtime (the growing season). The thing we need to comprehend is what these horses are representing in this grand dance. One good possibility is they were showing Black Elk all the people of every color who would be coming together from the four quarters of the world. As we get deeper into Black Elk's vision, this concept will begin to make more sense.

Black Elk:

The bay horse turned to Black Elk and said; *Look, notice how the horses are dancing.* He looked around and saw the sky filled with happy dancing horses of every color encircling him. *Hurry,* the bay said, so they walked alongside each other. The black, white, sorrel and buckskin horses followed behind marching four abreast.

Clarification:

This was Black Elk's first glimpse of a world without color barriers. This spiritual path states everything that is positive moves in a clockwise circle, starting with the blacks, whites, sorrels, and buckskin horses marching in a line four by four. Four is a sacred number; the four cycles of the seasons, the four directions, and the four colors of the horses, etc. Many Lakota believe the reason for the four colors is they represent the four main colors of humankind, black, red, yellow, and white.

Black Elk:

Black Elk noticed all the dancing horses turning into animals of every type and into every bird that was and flew back to where all the horses had come from, the west, north, east and south.

Clarification:

This statement takes us a little further in depth. The dancing horses of every color and without number changing into animals of every type and all the birds, is making a statement, "Mitakúye Oyasin." The fact they all returned to the four quarters from whence the horses came and vanished, bolsters the idea the Grandfathers were showing Black Elk his relationship with all things within the four quarters of the World. The Grandfathers would not establish this type of relationship and then exclude the wasichu. This will become more apparent as we move deeper into this vision.

Figure 3: Black Elk holding his ceremonial drum while Standing Bear holds Black Elk's Sacred Pipe.
Photograph taken by John G. Neihardt during the interview for *Black Elk Speaks.* **Courtesy John G. Neihardt Trust, Western Historical Manuscript Collection-Columbia.**

Chapter 7: The Six Grandfathers

The following is a summary account from John G. Neihardt's *Black Elk Speaks*, Chapter 3 The Great Vision.

Black Elk:

As Black Elk, the bay horse, the blacks, whites, sorrels and buckskin horses all marched; they came to a cloud shaped like a tepee with a rainbow for its door. When Black Elk looked through the rainbow door, he saw six old men (the Grandfathers) sitting inside. The two men that accompanied him now stood on each side with the blacks, whites, sorrels and buckskin horses facing in and standing in rows of four, with each group representing the four directions. The eldest Grandfather spoke to Black Elk in a gentle manner and said; *Enter and do not be afraid.* As the Grandfather was speaking, all the horses whinnied, showing their support for Black Elk. He entered the lodge and stood in front of the Six Grandfathers. They looked older than men of the earth could be. The eldest Grandfather said; *Your Grandfathers are having a gathering, and have sent for you, to instruct you.* Black Elk said he knew these were not just old men; they were the powers of the six directions, and he was frightened.

Clarification:

Before I continue with this vision, I would like to clarify the colors of the four directions. The traditional colors are black for the west; red for the north; yellow for the east; and white for the south. When Black Elk received his great vision, the spirits established the colors of the four directions by reversing white to the north, red to east and yellow to the south. They did not change the black in the west. What is important to understand is that when Black Elk shared his vision of the flowering tree with John G. Neihardt, Black Elk did not add to or take anything away from the original vision. It also sets his vision apart from others, as it should.

In another chapter, I will explain in detail a little more about the rainbow tepee and the origin of the Six Grandfathers. The two thunder beings that escorted Black Elk were his guardians and the blacks, whites, sorrels, and the buckskin horses stood in their four quarters facing in. The idea they faced in, shows they supported what was going on. If they had faced outward, they would have been rejecting the whole thing. The fifth and oldest Grandfather is Wakáŋ Táŋka (Great Spirit, God), or in its oldest translation meaning, the Great Mystery. [I like this meaning and will use it throughout the book because who can say what God is or even looks like, it is just that, a great mystery.]

Black Elk:

The first spirit is from the west; the second spirit is from the north; the third spirit is from the east; the fourth spirit is from the south. The eldest spirit is the fifth, that of the sky, the sixth spirit is that of the earth.

Clarification:

The first spirit is Grandfather of the West; the second spirit is Grandfather of the North; the third spirit is Grandfather of the East; the forth spirit is Grandfather of the South. The fifth spirit is Grandfather Great Mystery the oldest, that of the sky.

The sixth spirit is Grandfather Earth, also referred to as Grandmother Earth. Students have asked why Black Elk referred to the sixth Spirit as Grandfather, and not Grandmother. Spirit is both male and female; it is not about gender, as their energy has aspects of both male and female. The meaning of Grandfather or Grandmother represents the highest realm concerning sacred and spiritual respect; it is not about gender.

I have heard many hardened Lakota warriors say they were both man and woman. They are simply embracing their masculine and feminine aspects of who they are.

Black Elk:

Black Elk said he was frightened until the First Grandfather, he of the west, began speaking. He told Black Elk to look towards the west, the place of the thunder beings. From the thunder beings, Black Elk will have his power. He said the thunder beings would take Black Elk to the remote and lofty axis of the world where he could view the whole world, and then to the east, where the sun is always shining, they will take him there to find understanding and wisdom.

Clarification:

Now, the First Grandfather, the spirit of the west, spoke and said, 'Black Elk will have the power of the west, that of the thunder beings.' They would take him to Harney Peak (as of 2016 it was renamed Black Elk peak) the high and remote center of the earth to see the entire world. From this high summit, they will take him eastward where the sun is always shining and from there he will seek understanding and wisdom. At this point in Black Elk's vision, the Grandfather of the west confirmed Black Elk's powers of the west and the thunder beings will work through him as a Heyóka.

Black Elk:

The First Grandfather was speaking of Understanding when Black Elk saw a rainbow jump and soar over his head. The Grandfather held out a wooden cup filled with water. When Black Elk looked into the cup, he saw the sky. The Grandfather handed Black Elk the cup and said; *This is for you, the power of life.* He then handed Black Elk a bow and said; *This is for you; it has the power to destroy.*

Clarification:

Again, the flaming rainbow can represent all colors of the world coming together as one. It also represents the thunder beings from the west, bringing the rain that we may live, and the lightning that can destroy. In life, one does not exist without the other; it is called being in balance. What is important is when and how Black Elk uses these gifts, the wooden cup of water, the power of life, and the bow to destroy. As a Heyóka, these will be his powers.

Black Elk:

The First Grandfather told Black Elk he is his spirit and Black Elk was his body. His name is Eagle Wing Stretches. The First Grandfather got up and proceeded to run toward the west, then without warning he turned into a black horse. When the horse stopped, and looked at Black Elk, he was sick and starving with all his ribs showing.

The Second Grandfather, he of the north where the white giant lives, stood holding an herb in his hand and told Black Elk; *Quick, take this herb to the black horse.* Black Elk held the herb over the sick horse, and he quickly recovered and was shiny black, healthy, cheerful and returned to where he was sitting and changed back into the First Grandfather.

Clarification:

The Grandfather of the west declared that Black Elk is his earth-bound body and gave him his spirit name, Eagle Wing Stretches. A Medicine Man once told me, he does not know why people want an Indian name, they already have a name. He went on to say, "A spiritual name will come to you in a vision or an elder or a Medicine Man will give it to you. In the Lakota way, the spiritual name is not a given name; a spiritual name is for ceremony or when one passes into the spirit world."

The black horse that was sick and starving with all his ribs showing, and the herb the Second Grandfather of the North, gave to Black Elk is an important part of the vision. You might think the black horse was exhibiting physical starvation. The real culprit would not be as much about the lack of food as it would be about the lack of spirituality. The sick and starving black horse with his ribs showing is symbolic of the people falling away from their spiritual ways. The herb could have been sweet grass, single stem sage, or flat cedar, used when opening ceremonies. When Black Elk held the herb toward the black horse, the Grandfathers were showing him how to bring the spiritual path back to the people, so they may live a good spiritual life.

Black Elk:

The Grandfather of the north said; *Be brave younger brother; on earth a nation you will save.* He told Black Elk his power would be the white giant's wing, a purifying wind. After saying this, the Second Grandfather stood up and ran in the direction of the north; he turned and was a white goose standing there. When Black Elk looked around, he noticed in the west the horses were thunder beings, in the north, the horses were white geese.

Clarification:

The Second Grandfather affirmed Black Elk's relationship by addressing him as a younger brother. This is something familiar to Lakota, as they tend to address each other as younger brother, uncle, father, Grandfather, etc. Black Elk's power of the north would be the white giant's wing; the purifying wind, separating the good seeds from bad seeds, building endurance and courage. The people would lose this power and Black Elk would have to bring it back to them. The Second Grandfather represents the horses in the north that were white geese, while the First Grandfather represents the horses in the west that were thunder beings. When these two work together, they could produce thunder, lightning and snow at the same time or even a hailstorm. When these two Grandfathers are working together, we all take notice! The Heyóka usually wears black clothing with white spots; sometimes the clothing is black, white, with some red.

Black Elk:

The Third Grandfather, he of the east, the place where the sun always shines, began to speak: *Be brave younger brother, for over the earth they shall escort you.* With his hand, he motioned toward the morning star, and from below it, two men came, flying. The Grandfather told Black Elk he would have power from them, as they awaken everything with roots, legs or wings. The Grandfather held out a peace pipe with a spotted eagle stretched out on its stem. The eagle appeared to be alive as it sat quivering and with its eyes looking at Black Elk. The Grandfather said; *Across the earth you will carry this pipe and whoever sickens, you would heal.*

The Grandfather then motioned toward a man whose body was a brilliant red representing all things pleasant and abundant. The man dropped to the ground, rolled and then turned into a buffalo. He stood up and ran to where the sorrel horses were in the east, and they too became buffalo.

Clarification:

The Third Grandfather was of the east where the sun always shines, referring to the idea the sun is always shining no matter what area of the earth it is located. He also confirmed Black Elk's relationship and said he would have the power of the east. The two men flying were spirits of light that awaken all things of the earth with roots, legs and wings, bringing understanding and wisdom through light. The Third Grandfather presented Black Elk with the caŋnuŋpa and told him that with this pipe he would have the power of a medicine man to doctor all illnesses. The spotted eagle is important to the pipe as it flies the highest and will carry the prayers from the pipe to the Great Mystery.

The bright red man represents purity. The buffalo represents life force as everything the people needed came from the buffalo. Together the color red and the buffalo represent the Lakota spiritual way of life.

Black Elk received the rites of a Holy Man (Wicasa Wakáŋ) or Medicine Man (Wicasa Pejúta) from the Third Grandfather. Today our Medicine Men and Holy Men are pretty much one in the same; they both work with the pipe, herbs, and with spirit. From the First Grandfather, he of the West, Black Elk would have the powers of the Heyóka.

Black Elk:

The Fourth Grandfather, he of the south, the place we always face, began to speak. From this place is the power to grow. The forth Grandfather called Black Elk 'younger brother' and said he would have power from the four directions, and would be a relative to them.

He said; *Observe, I shall give to you the living center of the people, and with this, you will rescue many.* He noticed the forth Grandfather was holding a living, 'red stick.' As Black Elk looked, branches began to sprout from its end with leaves that rustled softly, and from its leaves, birds were singing. Black Elk said for just a moment he thought he saw his people's village circled around the base of the tree, with all living things with roots, legs and wings, and they all were joyful. The Grandfather said; *At the center of the people's circle it will grow, a staff to walk with and the heart of a people. And with your power, it will blossom.*

Clarification:

Again, the Fourth Grandfather, he of the south, confirmed Black Elk's relationship with the powers of the four directions. He gave Black Elk a red stick (the sacred color of purity). It also represented the spring, the growing season, and a tree that sprouts branches, leaves and singing birds. Today many Indian people believe the cottonwood tree is symbolic of the Tree of Life that stands at the center of the nation's circle at many of the

Sun Dances. A staff to walk with and the heart of a people suggest, when people walk the 'good red road,' their life's problems are a little easier to solve. Black Elk will have to nurture this idea of the blossoming tree as a symbol of the center of the nation's hoop, which holds the people together in unison.

Black Elk:

The Fourth Grandfather said; *Observe the world below!* So, Black Elk looked below and saw the nations hoop, at its center grew the sacred tree. Two roads intersected it, one red and one black. From the north through to the south, the 'red road' runs, a road of high spirituality. The Grandfather said; *And on this road, your people will travel. From the west through to the east, the black road runs, a frightful road of difficulty and war, also on this road your people will travel.* He went on to say; *While you travel upon the black road, you will have the power to destroy an enemy. In four ascents, you will travel over the earth with power.* Black Elk thought when the Grandfather spoke of four ascents, he meant Black Elk would live to see four generations. He told Neihardt in 1932, 'Now, I am seeing the third ascent.' The fourth Grandfather stood tall and ran to where the buckskins stood, and turned into an elk, and then they turned into elk, all standing in the south.

Clarification:

The red and 'black roads' are not physical roads. The 'red road' represents the Lakota spiritual way of life. When walking this road, the people connect with the light of the daybreak star of understanding and to the Six Grandfathers. When the people walk the 'black road,' they travel the road of darkness and misunderstanding, troubles, war, and the lack of a connection to the Six Grandfathers. When we travel the 'black road,' we have the power to destroy our enemy. With this power, one could damage their soul, turning it dark.

When the Fourth Grandfather and the buckskin horses turned into elk, they were representing long life, as Black Elk would live to see four generations.

Black Elk:

The Fifth Grandfather, the oldest that of the sky, spoke, referring to Black Elk as "my boy." He told Black Elk he had requested his presence and was glad he came. He showed Black Elk his power by turning into a spotted eagle soaring over him. *Observe,* he said; *All the wings in the air, the winds and stars would be a relative* [to Black Elk.] The Grandfather told Black Elk he would walk the earth with his power. The eagle flew above Black Elk's head flapping and then the sky was filled with happy wings all around him.

Clarification:

The Fifth Grandfather, the Great Mystery that of the sky, not only made Black Elk a relative, he affirmed that the spotted eagle was his messenger by turning into a spotted eagle hovering. He then made Black Elk a relative to all the winged ones, winds and stars.

The other point here is the Great Mystery said Black Elk would have his power to go across the earth. This gives even more credence to Black Elk's vision in that it would not be just for the Lakota nation; it was for all the nations of the world and future generations.

Black Elk:

The Sixth Grandfather, he of the earth, stood looking at Black Elk. He was old, his hair was silver, and his face in wrinkles, but only like men of the earth are old. As Black Elk looked at him, he thought he knew him somehow. The Sixth Grandfather began changing, slowly becoming younger until he was a boy. Black Elk knew it was himself and that the Sixth Grandfather was showing him all the years he would have in his future. When the Grandfather became old again, he called Black Elk 'his boy', and told him to be brave, as he would have his power, and he would need it, as his people of the earth will suffer greatly.

The Sixth Grandfather stood up and ran out through the rainbow door, with Black Elk following on his bay horse, the one that led him to the rainbow tepee.

Clarification:

The Sixth Grandfather, he of the earth, made Black Elk a relative. Some people believe Black Elk was the Sixth Grandfather. In reality, Black Elk was just a relative. Grandmother Earth is the traditional spirit of the sixth direction also called, Mother Earth. The sixth spirit was showing Black Elk we are born of the earth, and when we pass into the spirit world, our body returns to the earth, all things are a relative to Mother Earth, our spiritual Mother.

The Grandfather was also giving Black Elk a glimpse into the future when he grew backward in time; he was showing Black Elk he would live to see four generations. The Sixth Grandfather gave Black Elk his power, as it is of the earth and Black Elk will need it, for his people on earth will suffer greatly. Again, they used the term 'earth' to represent all the people of the world. He led Black Elk out of the rainbow tepee to help setup the next phase of his vision.

Black Elk:

The bay horse stood facing the west, where the black horses stood, when Black Elk heard a voice say; *They gave you the wooden cup of water, the power of life the green day. They also gave you a bow and arrow, the power of death and destruction.* When the bay horse whinnied, the twelve black horses lined up behind the bay in rows of four, marching side by side.

Clarification:

As Black Elk prepared to begin the next phase of his journey, the Grandfather of the West confirmed the gifts he had given earlier: the wooden cup of water that sustains life, awakening all the beings of the earth, representing the green day. He was also given the bow and arrow that brings death and destruction. Again, the cup of water and the bow and arrow represent balance between the positive and negative forces.

Black Elk:

The bay horse stood facing the north, where the twelve white horses stood, when a voice said; *They have given you the power of the white giant's wing, a purifying wind and the sacred herb.* When the bay horse whinnied, the twelve white horses lined up behind the black horses in rows of four, marching side by side.

Clarification:

The spirit of the north confirmed the gifts he gave Black Elk: the sacred herb and the white giant's wing. Again, the sacred herb opens ceremonies and displaces all negative energies. The white giant's wing represents the cold snow and wind that blows across the earth, building strength and endurance separating good seeds from bad seeds.

The statement separating good seeds from bad seeds requires an explanation. When we look at what is going on in nature, it is easy to understand how the white giant's wing would separate good seeds from bad seeds as only the strong can survive in nature. This process ensures that every species reaches its potential or becomes extinct. Only the two legged has slipped out of the grasp of the white giant. As two-legged, we protect the sick and the weak living out our lives in the comfort of our air-conditioned homes. When Black Elk was growing up, the Lakota struggled to survive as life was hard and so were the Lakota. The Lakota, along with other tribes, were in harmony with nature. Today, much of our society has become soft; we are not as tough as we used to be, avoiding all contact with nature.

It is not my suggestion that we stop taking care of the sick and weak, for that is who we are as humans. What I am suggesting is that if you are healthy enough, then try venturing out into our State and National Parks and try to reconnect a little with nature. Shovel some snow, create a snowman, or snow angels with the kids. The point in all this is to embrace the white giant's wing; it will make you stronger and build endurance.

Black Elk:

The bay horse stood facing the east, where the sorrel horses stood; their foreheads had the morning star upon them, glowing brightly. Again, Black Elk heard a voice say; *They gave you the sacred pipe that is peace and the red day.* When the bay horse whinnied, the twelve sorrel horses lined up behind the white horses in rows of four, marching side by side.

Clarification:

The Grandfather of the East confirmed the gift he had given earlier: the sacred pipe. The idea the Grandfather states the pipe is for peace suggests that only positive prayers are placed into the pipe. The pipe is not to bring war or harm; it is used to bring peace and to heal the sick. When the Lakota signed a treaty, they smoked the pipe. In doing this, they would not break the treaty, as they would not defy the pipe. This is the reason the wasichu called the caŋnuŋpa, the peace pipe. The red day and the morning star represent the power of the east, understanding, and wisdom.

Black Elk:

The bay horse stood facing the south where the twelve buckskins horses stood when a voice said; *You have the power of the red stick, the nation's hoop and the yellow day. In the center of the hoop, you will plant the red stick. With your power, you will help it to grow into a*

64

blossoming tree. When the bay horse whinnied, the twelve buckskin horses lined up behind the sorrel horses in rows of four, marching side by side.

Clarification:

The Grandfather of the South confirmed the gift he had given earlier: the sacred red stick and the nation's hoop. Black Elk's responsibility will be to find the center of the hoop, and plant the stick and make it bloom. By doing this he will bring spirituality back to the people, the 'good red road'. The yellow day represents the growing power of the south. The way the twelve black horses, white horses, sorrel horses and buckskin horses line up in rows of four behind the bay is important to the vision. First, the number twelve represents the twelve moons and secondly, the number four (horses lined up in rows of four) represents the four seasons and or the four directions. As we get further into the vision, it will become more apparent just how Black Elk finds the center of the nation's hoop.

Black Elk:

Black Elk said he knew there were warriors on all the horses lined up behind him when a voice said; *You will travel upon the black road with all the mounted riders behind you. Behold, the two-legged, four-legged, rooted and winged will all fear you.* He traveled east upon the 'black road', with the four-horse troop following behind him, the blacks, whites, sorrel's and buckskin's. On this frightful road, he saw the Morning star in the east, rising in a faint light. As Black Elk and the four-horse troop passed overhead, he looked down and saw the earth in a nauseous green haze. All things looked up in fear, the hills, the rooted ones, animals of all kinds, and all the birds were taking flight.

Black Elk said he was the chief of the heavens and behind him; the twelve black horses were diving and rolling, making thunder; hail flew from their swirling manes and tales, and lightning flashed from their nostrils. As Black Elk rode above the earth, he saw the hail and biting rain falling to the

65

earth. He said the trees were bending and the hills grew dark, when they passed over, the earth became bright and green once again.

Clarification:

The Grandfather of the west told Black Elk that as you travel the 'black road' with your gifts, all things would fear you. The 'black road' is the road of troubles and war. When we are on this road, the light of the Morning star would be extremely dim, lacking understanding and wisdom. When we think about it, we seek shelter when a thunderstorm approaches. The twelve black horses represent the thunder beings; their swirling manes and tails represent the most feared, a tornado, and their nostrils flashed lightning. After they passed over the earth, it was bright again, as rain and lightning bring much needed nourishment to all things on earth, a cleansing. Remember, without the thunder beings we could not exist on this earth.

Black Elk:

Black Elk came to a place where three rivers joined, making one large river. He saw something there that was horrible; flames were everywhere and in the center of the flames lived a blue man. Dust filled the air, the grass and trees were drooping, the two-legged and four-legged were sick and fading, and birds too tired to fly.

Clarification:

The source where the three rivers came together is the three forks of the Missouri River. (I will write more about the subject of the flames and the blue man as we move deeper into the vision.)

Black Elk:

The black horse riders cried "Hoka hey", as they all dove down to strike at the blue man and were defeated. Then the white horse riders cried, diving down on the blue man and they too were defeated. Next, the sorrel horse riders and then the Buckskin horse riders also faced defeat by the blue man.

Clarification:

The term "Hoka hey!" is used to rally the hunters, to start an attack, to make ready, to draw others attention, or to just get moving along. Sometimes a drought is so severe it takes months for the thunder beings to break through.

Black Elk:

After the blue man drove them off, the four-horse troop shouted for Black Elk to attack. As he prepared for the attack, he heard many voices applauding him, so he dove down upon the blue man. In his right hand, he held the wooden cup of water, in his left hand, the bow. As he plunged downward, the bow became a lance with jagged lightning coming from its tip. As it struck the blue man's heart, Black Elk heard thunder and voices everywhere saying; *He has killed.* As the flames subsided, the grass and trees stood tall, the two-legged and four-legged cried with happiness, with birds singing in the trees. The warriors riding the blacks, whites, sorrels and buckskin horses dove down upon the blue man and struck him counting coup, and then the blue man changed into an innocent turtle.

Black Elk was riding in a storm cloud and came as rain. He said, with the power the Six Grandfathers gave him, he could kill the drought.

Clarification:

The wooden cup of water represented rain; the bow that turned into a lance represented the lightning. With these, Black Elk could end the drought. Spirits give the Heyóka knowledge to create a ceremony that can break up high-pressure systems to bring rain. [I cannot write about how they conduct this ceremony, as it is not mine to speak about. I will say, I have witnessed this ceremony and the results were astonishing.]

Now for the blue man, I have heard many non-Indian and some Indian people state they think the blue man represents the US Calvary. As Black Elk stated, it was drought he had defeated, not the U.S. Calvary. Within the flames a blue man lived, the heart and hottest part of the flame; take the blue flame away and the fire will die. When a warrior strikes an enemy with the back of their bow or coup stick, it represents the bravest of warriors, as they need to get in close, strike the enemy counting coup, and then ride off. The Grandfathers were showing Black Elk how to strike at the heart of a drought, (the blue man) the high-pressure system. The innocent turtle represents fertility.

Black Elk:
Black Elk rode into the village with the black, white, sorrel and buckskin riders behind him. Throughout the village, people were groaning and grieving for the dying and the dead, as a searing wind came out of the south. As he looked into the tepees, he saw men, women and children, sick and dying.

Black Elk felt sad as they rode through the village attending to the sick and dying. When he looked back, the men, women and children followed, with bright smiles on their faces. Black Elk heard a voice say; *Observe the center of a nation's hoop they have given you to bring to life.*

Clarification:
Remember the black horse, poor and sick. Black Elk healed him with the herb of power. When Black Elk rode through the village with the four-horse troops, he was not witnessing the physical sickness and starvation of the people. He was experiencing their spiritual death and depression. The sight of Black Elk along with the four-horse troops gave the people hope; they got up from their spiritual depression and came back to their spiritual

way of life. The voice said; *Observe, the center of a nation's hoop they have given you to bring to life.* Meaning, the people he had just saved from a spiritual death had given him the center of the nation's hoop, for without spiritual people the nation's hoop could not exist. It would be Black Elk's responsibility to make the blossoming tree bloom so the people could continue their spiritual way of life. With the return of their spiritual traditions, the Lakota would be able to pass these traditional teachings down to future generations.

Black Elk:

Black Elk and the four-horse troop moved to the center of the village. The four-horse troop took their places in the four directions circling around Black Elk. As the men, women and children began to congregate around Black Elk, a voice said; *Give them the flowering red stick so they may thrive, the sacred pipe that they will know peace, and the white giant's wing to create endurance and courage.* As Black Elk stood in the center of the nation's hoop, he pushed the red stick into the earth and it rapidly became a Waġa Caŋ; the rustling tree, lofty with many branches and leaves, and in the leaves, birds of all kinds were singing.

Clarification:

The four-horse troop positioned themselves in the four directions: the blacks in the west; whites in the north; sorrels in the east; and buckskins in the south, all looking inward, approving, and supporting the powers of the four directions. At this point, the Great Mystery instructed Black Elk to give the people the gift of the flowering red stick that the Grandfather of the south gave him. With the flowering stick, the people can find their way back to their spiritual way of life. Without their spiritual way of life, the people would be lost.

Black Elk also gave the people the gift the Grandfather of the north gave, the white giant's wing creating endurance and courage; and the gift of the sacred pipe, the Grandfather of the east gave, so the people would find peace. You should note the cup of water and the bow remain Black Elk's power of the Heyóka, used only when the people needed this power. The bright red stick Black Elk thrust into the ground turned into a Waǧa Caŋ (the cottonwood). As mentioned earlier, the cottonwood to this day, sits at the center of the nation's hoop at annual Sun Dance ceremonies.

Black Elk:

Below this grand tree, the animals were mingling with the people like relatives and making happy cries. All the people came together like family, like relatives shouting with joy. Women sounded their joyful tremolo, while the men cried out: 'In this place, we will raise the children like chicks under the Śiyó's wing.'

Clarification:

The animals mingling with the people like relatives, represents the relationship with all things. The woman's tremolo is the tremulous effect produced by rapid repetition of a single tone. Chicks sleep under the Śiyó's (Prairie Hen) wing for warmth and shelter. The mother hen is protective of the young, until they are old enough to take care of themselves. Grandmother Earth represents the mother Śiyó's wing protecting and providing for the people.

Black Elk:

As the Morning Star rose in the east a voice proclaimed; *It will be like a relative, those that see it will understand more, henceforth comes wisdom; those that do not seek the Morning star will be dark, henceforth comes ignorance.* Black Elk saw the people turn toward the east as the light of the Morning Star fell upon their faces, all things cried with joy.

Clarification:

Symbolically, when we participate in the Inipi (sweat lodge) ceremony and the door to the lodge is closed, you are plunged into darkness; you find yourself ignorant of all things around you. This is a time to be serious in our prayers. When the door to the lodge is opened, you are surrounded by light and become aware of all things around you, understanding and wisdom, it is a time to be joyful. Four times, we close the door where we experience darkness and ignorance, at the end of each round, we open the door to remind us to work with the light of the Morning Star (Venus). Intention is everything when it comes to seeking true spiritual meaning.

The idea of standing in the dark every morning, waiting for the Morning Star to rise, is the intention that reaches to the depth of our soul that states you seek wisdom and understanding. When we do not reach for the light of the morning star, we lack understanding and wisdom, and our soul is dark. Many Lakota greet the Morning Star at sunrise to begin their day.

Black Elk:

When all was still again a great voice said; *Observe the hoop of the nation, it is holy and without end, as within the power of the people all powers shall be one never-ending.*

Clarification:

The great Voice was that of the Great Mystery, stating the nation's hoop represents all the people, the seventh direction. Together, they pray as spiritual beings, a powerful unity without end. The concept that all nations with their cultural and religious differences will be coming together as one, is thought provoking. This concept will become clearer as we continue along this vision.

Figure 4: Photo taken at the Memorial Room, John G. Neihardt Center, Bancroft, NE. Shown, is Black Elk's Drum, his Sacred Pipe and the symbol of the Nations Hoop. Courtesy Ginger Young

When Black Elk shared his Great Vision with John G. Neihardt, he allowed Neihardt to write about it in the book, *Black Elk Speaks*. Furthermore, he gave Neihardt the natural world gifts that represent the gifts of his Great Vision. The Wooden Cup and Bow/Arrows from the Grandfather of the West. The White Wing and Healing Herb from the Grandfather of North. The Sacred Pipe of peace from the Grandfather of East, and the Bright Red Stick and Nations Hoop from the Grandfather of the South.

He also gave Neihardt his Ceremonial Drum; all these gifts are shown in the Memorial Room of the Neihardt Center. The Bow/Arrows were kept with the Neihardt Trust, as they felt these items represented Black

Elk's power of the Wakíyaŋ Oyáte: (Thunder Being People). Out of respect for Black Elk and his Great Vision the Bow/Arrows were not displayed in the Memorial Room with the other gifts.

On August 2, 2015 Ginger and I were honored to have been invited to attend the 50th anniversary of the John G. Neihardt Center. During this ceremony, the Neihardt family returned the Bow/Arrows to the Black Elk family.

Chapter 8: The Caŋnuŋpa (Pipe) Doctoring

The following is a summary account from John G. Neihardt's *Black Elk Speaks*, Chapter 3 The Great Vision,

Black Elk:

The Third Grandfather, he of the east - the place where the sun always shines- began to speak. Be brave younger brother, for over the earth they shall escort you. With his hand, he motioned toward the morning star, and from below it, two men came, flying. The Grandfather told Black Elk he would have power from them, as they awaken everything with roots, legs or wings. The Grandfather held out a peace pipe with a spotted eagle stretched out on its stem. The eagle appeared to be alive as it sat quivering and with its eyes looking at Black Elk. The Grandfather said; *Across the earth you will carry this pipe and whoever sickens, you would heal.*

Black Elk's First Doctoring

The following is a summary account from John G. Neihardt's *Black Elk Speaks*, Chapter 17, The First Cure.

In 1882 at age nineteen, Black Elk performed his first doctoring with the pipe. Black Elk and his friend One Side found an herb growing in the edge of a clay gulch. The herb was flowering in the four colors, blue, white, red, and yellow. Black Elk said he had never seen such an herb before, except in his vision. After offering red willow bark and praying about it, he dug up the herb to use as his personal medicine.

The next day a man named Cuts-to-Pieces petitioned Black Elk with a pipe asking him to heal his son who was extremely sick and would soon die without help. Using the herb, a wooden cup of water, his pipe, and the young daughter of Cuts-To-Pieces, Black Elk performed the doctoring ceremony. After four days, the sickness lifted and boy could eat, drink and walk again.

Fast Horse and the Pipe

Diagnosed with cancer in 1977, Dr. Gillihan underwent a series of operations and chemotherapy. His weight dropped from 240 lbs. to 116 lbs. In 1978, the doctors told Dr. Gillihan there was nothing more they could do for him and that he should get his papers in order. Frank Fools Crow remembered his good friend and sent Charles Fast Horse and his brother to conduct a pipe ceremony at the hospital where Dr. Gillihan stayed.

Fast Horse received permission to conduct the pipe ceremony in Dr. Gillihan hospital room and during the filling of the pipe ceremony little lights appeared outside his window. When they came into the room, the little lights entered Dr. Gillihan through both his nipples and then exited from his bellybutton. They hovered in front of Fast Horse for a moment and then exited back out through the window. Fast Horse looked over at him and said, "This is a tough one, it will take four days, and then you will be okay."

On the fourth day, the nurse drew blood for the lab to check the cancer tracers. After the third try, the doctor came into the room with the nurse and said there seems to be a problem reading the blood draws, so I need to make sure we are drawing the blood in the correct manner. Later that day the doctor came back into Dr. Gillihan's room and said, "we cannot find any cancer tracers in your blood, the cancer is gone." The doctors asked

Dr. Gillihan if Fast Horse could go to all the rooms and he said it would not work unless one truly believes in the power of the pipe and prayer.

In the latter part of 1978 while recovering from his bout with cancer, he drove to South Dakota to thank his friend and teacher Frank Fool's Crow. Fool's Crow asked him to carry one of Sitting Bull's pipes and use it to pray for the people each year. Dr. Gillihan became the fourth Keeper of the Sitting Bull Pipe, and carried the pipe with humble dignity in service for all the people for the next twenty-four years.

The Doctoring of Peter

In the winter of 1993, Kathy and I set up three speaking engagements for Fast Horse in the Chicago area. He and his family were staying at my home, in Channahon, Illinois. One evening, a friend brought his son Peter to my home to meet Fast Horse. Peter, a ten-year-old boy diagnosed with terminal brain cancer wanted to meet Fast Horse.

Fast Horse sat looking at Peter and said, "I understand you have a problem, is there anything I can do for you!" Peter said, "I have cancer in the brain stem and the doctors have not been able to cure me." Fast Horse sat studying him for a moment and then said, "Would you like me to take the cancer away?" "Yes please", said Peter.

Fast Horse reached for his pipe bag and began to remove the pipe bowl, pipe stem, and other items from the bag. He asked if we would light some sage to purify the room and all those that were present. He began setting items out onto a large piece of red cloth and then assembled the pipe stem to the bowl. He lit some sweet grass and began filling his pipe and praying in the Lakota language. When he had finished filling the pipe, he had Peter stand in front of him where he used an eagle fan to wipe him down, starting at his head and moving down to his feet. Fast Horse lit the pipe, blowing smoke over him and then finished smoking the pipe.

After everyone left for the evening, Fast Horse said, "In four days the spirits will come here to start the doctoring." Fast Horse and his wife were staying in my bedroom, his cousin John and wife were in the spare bedroom and two Lakota men and I slept in the living room. The house was quite full at this point.

On the evening of the fourth night at about 12:00 am, awakened by a crackling sound, we noticed colorful lights dancing all around the room. Without warning, as if we were in an earthquake, the walls began to shake, and the hanging pictures began rattling against the wall. Fast Horse yelled to us saying, "Quick, light some sage". After lighting the sage, the room began to settle down, and Fast Horse came out of the bedroom looking somewhat pale.

He sat down on a bench seat located along the southern wall of the living room and asked if anyone knew of any ancient Indian burial mounds located in the Channahon area. I told him there were some Pottawatomie mounds less than a mile from here, along the Kankakee River. Fast Horse said, "There is a chief buried in a large mound, he came here tonight and was standing at the foot of the bed wearing a chief's headdress with the feathers standing straight up in a circle. In the center of this headdress was a long-necked bird that seemed to be alive, looking all-around the room. He was wearing a highly-decorated robe and holding a long staff."

He went on to say, "This chief walked over to the closet and was looking at something. Do you have your pipe bundle in the closet?" I answered, "Yes, I keep the pipe in the closet, away from curious eyes."

He said, "I think he was looking at your pipe, and then he came back over to the foot of the bed, reached out with his staff and touched me. It felt like a bolt of static electricity, and then the bed began to shake and then, he was gone". I asked why this spirit lit him up that way; he just smiled and said the chief was just showing me who was in charge. He was here to help with the doctoring, as Peter also lives in Channahon.

Fast Horse said, "Peter has some things to work out in his life; it will be your responsibility to help him accomplish this. You should plan to spend as much time with him as possible. The cancer will not continue to spread while he is working through his concerns, and then the doctoring will be complete; he will be okay."

For the next year and a half, I worked with Peter teaching him about the arts, with respect to the Lakota art. His area of interest would be the dream catcher, and he mastered the concept. He spent hours weaving dream catchers, with each one having its own personality. Before long, they became highly sought after by collectors. The arts seemed to give him meaning, and slowly he opened up, and began talking about the things that concerned him.

In the summer of 1994, my eight-year-old daughter Samantha, Peter, and his mother and I traveled to the Black Hills to visit the sacred sites. On one of our stops, we met up with Dr. Gillihan at the Crazy Horse Memorial. He understood what Peter was going through with respect to the pipe doctoring and spent some quiet time talking about the meaning of the pipe and its meaning to Peter. Dr. Gillihan reached into his bag of sacred items and handed him an old medicine bag of his, telling Peter to keep it close to him, as it holds good spiritual medicine.

The following day Samantha, Peter, his mother and I headed for Bear Butte. A thunderstorm was coming fast from the west so we decided to return to the car. I said, "Do not worry, this is Bear Butte, the thunder beings are just coming to purify it."

My daughter said, "Oh, okay Dad," and then she began walking even faster toward the car. Over the years, I remember reading and hearing stories of thunder beings flying in the storm clouds. Huge eagles with lightning coming from their eyes and thunder from the flapping of their wings. I always thought that was a bit of a stretch, until we experienced this phenomenon for ourselves.

As we were walking, I was thinking it would be nice if the thunder beings could show the kids who they are, so they would not be so frightened. At that moment, we noticed the clouds began to change their shape into huge wings. It was like an oil painting in the sky with all the feathers, even the long tip feathers spreading out. One wing passed over us, stretching out for about a half mile and the other wing equally as long passed over the Butte. It was incredible as it flew backwards over us with lightning coming from the area of its head. There was a soft gentle rain, and then it was gone.

The kids were enamored by the site of this and their fear just melted away. I did not consider this a vision. The idea that the Thunder Being heard my thoughts and showed kindness toward all of us, caused me to feel exceptionally small.

A few months after returning to Channahon, Peter returned to the hospital to check on the progress of his cancer. What they found was his cancer was gone. As of this writing, Peter turned thirty years old and has become an accomplished artist. I often wonder if Dr. Gillihan's gift and the coming of the thunder being at Bear Butte was the final part of the doctoring for Peter.

Another use for the pipe is the marriage ceremony. In August 2001, Dr. Gillihan used the Sitting Bull pipe to unite Ginger and me in a Lakota wedding ceremony; it was the last time he would use the pipe before his spirit journey on June 7, 2002.

The seven rites of the Oglala Sioux are ceremonies within the pipe. The first and oldest rite is the Inipi (purification, sweat lodge). The second rite is Haŋbleceya (crying for a vision, or vision quest). The third rite is Wiwaŋ'yag Wachi'pi (the Sun Dance). The fourth rite is Keeping and releasing of the Soul. The fifth rite is Huŋkápi (making of a relative). The sixth rite is Ishŋa Ta Awi Cha Lowaŋ (coming into womanhood), and the seventh rite is Tapa Waŋká Yap (throwing of the ball).

As with all seven rites, and other ceremonies, there is always a pipe on the altar. [If you wish to get a better understanding of the seven rites of the pipe, I suggest you read *The Sacred Pipe: Black Elk's account of the seven rites of the Oglala Sioux.* by Joseph Epes Brown.

Chapter 9: Vision at Needle's Eye

It was mid July 1995, when Devin Smith, a Black Foot friend, my daughter, Samantha, and I set out for the Black Hills of South Dakota. This would be my sixth annual pilgrimage to the sacred sites within the Black Hills. Our campsite was in the hills not far from Keystone, South Dakota where we would fill and smoke our pipes to begin the prayers. The following day we would spend time filling our pipes on Bear Butte, and then finish the day by climbing to the top of the Butte as I have done every year since. The last three days of our pilgrimage would be at Gray Horn Butte, also known as Devil's Tower.

This year we felt we should include Harney Peak as the third site to pray with our pipes. The idea was to create balance, instead of just filling pipes at our campsite, Bear Butte and Gray Horn Butte. After filling and smoking our pipes at the campsite, we made plans to head for Bear Butte the following day to establish the second site. On the third day, we packed a lunch, and headed out for the third site at Harney Peak. The trip would take us through Keystone past Mount Rushmore on Route 244 to Highway 16 toward Custer and Route 87 (called Needle's Highway). While driving on Route 87, we came upon a steep grade with four switchbacks. Once we completed these tight turns at the top of this hill, we entered a narrow tunnel before reaching the Custer State Park Ranger Station located by Sylvan Lake.

Somehow, while looking for the entrance to Harney Peak, we ended up at a place called "Needle's Eye," a circular drive with two entrances, one from the northwest and the other from the east that passed through a one-lane tunnel. The circular drive is about 60 to 70 feet in diameter, having six huge 30 to 40-foot-tall granite monoliths standing around the edges of the circle including the monolith formation called, Needle's Eye.

We found ourselves standing amid fifty tourists taking pictures and climbing all over these formations. We could not shake the idea that this was the place we should be filling our pipes. The last thing I wanted to do would be to put on a show for a bunch of tourists, so we began looking around for a quiet place to fill the pipes, away from all the noise and curious eyes. We found a path just outside the northwest entrance that wound uphill opposite the Needle's Eye formation, and began to climb the steep trail. We came to a small, flat clearing that butted up against a large rock formation. By this time, the sound of laughter and screaming children was down to a manageable muffle. When we turned to look back at the granite monoliths, we found ourselves looking across at the tops of these natural rock formations. (See Figures 5, 6 and 7)

What we saw was utterly astonishing. At the top of these granite monoliths were faces of old men looking upward. After studying these for some time, we purified everything in our pipe bundles and ourselves with sage smoke. We assembled our pipe bowls to the stems and commenced to draw in sage smoke to purify the entire pipe before the filling ceremony. Unexpectedly, both pipes plugged up; we could not blow out or draw inward. This was incredibly odd as we always clean our pipes after each use. I sat looking at Devin and said, "I think this place has a problem with us." I began to think about how we proceeded at the other sites and realized we had not introduced ourselves or even asked permission to smoke our pipes and pray with the spirits of this special place.

With heartfelt apologies, we both explained why we were there and what our intent was. I heard a soft voice say; *Hold a lit match over the bowl of your pipe, and draw in.* I did this and the pipe cleared, and I blew out a puff of black smoke. Devin repeated the procedure with the same results, clearing his pipe as well. At this point, we felt confident and began filling our pipes. Just then, my daughter Samantha got up and began walking down the hill. My immediate thought was to tell her not to leave, when a voice said; *She will be all right; let her go.* We finished filling our pipes and then smoked them in this strange place.

As we were cleaning our pipes and putting things away, Samantha came back to the clearing. She had a little grin on her face and when I asked where she had gone, she said, "I was walking down the hill and saw a 12-or 13-year old boy walking up the trail, so I hid behind a large rock that had a small split in it. I could see him but he could not see me, when something told me to roll a small stone down the trail. I did this and the boy stopped, looked at the stone bouncing past him with some confusion. I had a feeling I should growl loudly, so I did. It was real funny to watch this boy running down the hill, screaming and yelling for his mom." I guess the spirits of this place have a good sense of humor. Moreover, Samantha did prevent him from walking up on our pipe ceremony.

We returned to our campsite, setup a fire in the stone pit, ate dinner, and just sat back, enjoying the energy of this place before retiring for the evening.

Figure 5: Thunder Being looking up, it is located to
the right of the tunnel at the eastern entrance. Notice
the lance tip at left side, tucked under his chin.

Figure 6: Needle's Eye monolith

**Figure 7: Waŋblí Gleška, the Spotted Eagle that came with
the pipe the Third Grandfather gave Black Elk. It is
located on the left side, below guardrail.**

The following morning, Devin got up around 5:00 am, lit a fire in the stone pit, and prepared a pot of coffee. I was hoping to get a little more sleep, but gave up after ten minutes of Devin's noisiness and then joined him. As for Samantha, she could sleep through a hurricane. It was just before dawn and quite cool that morning, as we sat around the fire while waiting for the coffee to boil.

Sitting on the south side of the fire pit on a park bench, I warmed myself by the fire while Devin sat on our cooler on the north side of the pit. The fire pit was made of stones piled about eight inches high in a circle of about three feet in diameter. Devin was eating a breakfast roll when he noticed a little sparrow sitting on the ground in the west about ten feet away. Devin broke off a piece of his roll, threw it over by the bird, and said, "Why don't you join us for breakfast little guy."

The sparrow hopped over, ate the piece of roll, then proceeded to walk to where I was sitting, and stood between my feet with his back to me. I said, "This is a bizarre little bird." At that moment, he turned his head and looked up into my eyes. His eyes were strange looking and I commented they were like those of a Grandfather—like the eyes of an old man. He then turned his head to face the fire pit and moved up against my left foot, tucked his beak into his chest, and took a nap. While he napped, I spoke with Devin about the weird behavior of this bird, taking care not to move my left foot. He had no fear of me or the hot fire, burning just a couple of feet away. I think he must have napped for about fifteen minutes before waking up and then walking clockwise around the fire pit towards where Devin was sitting.

When he arrived in the north end of the fire pit, he walked in be-tween Devin's feet, turned his head, and looked up into Devin's eyes. He sat looking at the bird and said: "This is a Grandfather." Then the sparrow turned his head to face the pit and took another nap. It was not a long nap, maybe 5 minutes or so before he hopped up onto Devin's left foot. Devin was wearing black sneakers with one drop of red paint on the toe of the left shoe. The Sparrow pecked at the red spot two times, looked up at Devin, and then hopped off, continuing to walk clockwise around the fire pit.

On the south side of pit was a flat stone, one inch thick, four inches wide, and six inches long, resting on top of the pit with its long side pointing inward toward the fire. For some reason, I picked up the stone and turned it so that its long side was in line with the circular pit. Now this is where things got bizarre. As the bird reached the south end of the pit where I was sitting, he began climbing up onto the top of the pit with a hot fire burning at its center. He then stepped onto the flat stone I had just repositioned and began hopping repeatedly, picking up his left foot, then his right foot, for a couple of minutes.

88

As I watched this funny little dance, I thought to myself, if the stone was so hot, maybe he should get off- only to remember I had just touched the stone myself and it was not hot. The sparrow continued hopping for another thirty seconds or so, before jumping backward off the fire pit. Once on the ground he walked in-between my feet and took another nap. This time, it was a short nap lasting less than a minute; he turned his head, looked up at me, and then began walking back toward the west of the pit from whence he came. Just then, two Robins flew in and landed about thirty feet from us in the west. The sparrow ran up to them as if they were his parents but they chased him away. He flew up and over the fire pit and disappeared into the east. Both Devin and I were at a loss for words. What in the world was that all about? We knew something had just played out, but were clueless as to its meaning.

One point worth mentioning is, when things act out of the ordinary, this is the time to pay attention. Spirits will use anything- including a sparrow- to get our attention.

The following day, we set out for Gray Horn Butte to spend a few days camping and taking our pipes to the west side of the Butte for the last of our four pipe ceremonies. I always feel a little melancholy when I must leave the Black Hills, but I needed to get back to work and participate in the world of humankind.

One month later, I was reading an article written by John Edgar Wideman for Modern Maturity. He had interviewed an American Indian about his reason for the Sun Dance. It was like a download of information, and then I understood what the sparrow was telling us. Devin and I must prepare to Sun Dance.

A couple of weeks later I spoke with two American Indian elders, Dr. Gillihan and Earl Meshiguad, about the sparrow vision. They both confirmed that this is exactly how they show you. Earl was helpful in describing each movement of the Sparrow.

My response to him was that it is my intent to prepare for the rest of the year and then make the Sun Dance in July. I went on to say, piercing to the Sun Dance tree was not in my plan, but I would make the dance, even at the ripe old age of 51. Earl said, "Do you remember when the bird pecked twice at the red spot on Devin's left sneaker? At the Sun Dance, you will apply two spots of wet red pipe stone dust onto your chest, that way the Medicine Man will know where to pierce you, insert the two wooden pins, and connect them to the harness hanging from the tree. When the sparrow jumped off the pit backward, he was showing you how to break free from the tree."

Sitting there with a perplexed look on my face, I said, "The Sun Dance would have been a lot more fun at 20 years old, than starting the dance at 51. Funny they (spirits) waited until now to give me a vision to start the dance." Earl just looked at me, smiled, and said, "If you dance with all the energy you have to give, the Sun Dance will keep you young and strong."

On the day, the sparrow came to Devin and me, we just observed its strange behavior. If we had tried to reach down to pick it up, it would have flown away and our vision to Sun Dance would have been lost to us.

Chapter 10: The Rainbow Tepee

It was in mid-June 1996, when Devin and I returned to the Black Hills to repeat our pipe ceremonies at the four sacred sites. What made this trip different is we had invited seven friends to join us. Devin and I setup our camp in the same place as the year before, and the rest of the group set their camps nearby. This would be my seventh annual pilgrimage to the sacred sites within the Black Hills. At this campsite, we filled and smoked our pipes to begin the prayers. The following morning, we took our pipes onto Bear Butte to establish the second site to fill our pipes. When we returned to our base camp, everyone sat around the fire pit, talking about the third site, Needle's Eye.

Devin needed to petition a spiritual leader and elder as a request to put him out on a Vision Quest before he could Sun Dance. The elder was staying in the Black Hills at a motel in Custer, South Dakota; a fifty-minute trip, and it was getting late. Devin and I arrived at 11:45 pm to find the group getting ready to call it a night. The elder was a kind man and agreed to take Devin's petition with his pipe, which meant when he smoked the pipe, he agreed to put Devin out for his Vision Quest.

After visiting with the elder for about thirty minutes, we headed back to our campsite. The trip would take us north on Highway 16 to Route 244, east past Mount Rushmore and through the town of Keystone, then left on Route 40 for about one mile. This was our plan but as things would have it, we would find ourselves on a dark and winding road. It was so dark that it swallowed up the headlights of our car. We had no idea where we were, we just kept driving. My thoughts were, we would eventually run into Highway 16 as it made one big circle that wrapped around the Black Hills. Devin seemed a little uncomfortable with this dark road, so I took the opportunity to say, "Wouldn't it be cool if Crazy Horse were to jump out onto the road right now." Devin looked over at me and said, "Stop it that was not cool!" Who would have believed this Black Foot dude was afraid of the dark?

Oh well, that was the only real fun part of this drive when without warning, the road ended at a granite wall. I slammed on the brakes, stopping the car about two feet from the wall. We sat there looking at this wall for what seemed to be a full minute, before I said, "What kind of an idiot Engineer designs a road that ends into a wall?" We agreed the best course of action would be to try to turn around and go back the way we came, wherever that was. As I began backing up, I slowly turned the car to my left, when the headlights fell into an opening that appeared to be a cave. We noticed a goat standing in the entrance of this cave, just looking at us. He turned and began walking into the cave, when a voice said, *Follow the goat*. So, I did what any reasonable person would do, and slowly drove in and followed the goat. As I proceeded to drive into the cave, I noticed the floor seemed flat enough, with adequate room on both sides and top of the car, so I continued.

We followed the goat until we exited the cave at the far end only to find ourselves back on another road. At this point, we were extremely confused. Our decision was to turn around, go back through the cave, and try to find our way back to Hwy 16. As I made the hard-left turn, we noticed the goat was standing on a ledge about three feet off the roadbed. Just then, we noticed what we originally thought was a cave, was not a cave at all, it was a tunnel. In that instant, it was like vertigo. How could we have confused a tunnel for a cave and why would I even try to drive into a cave? As we prepared to drive back through the tunnel, I realized where we were. We had arrived at the Needle's Eye; the tunnel was the eastern entrance. (See Figure 8 and 9)

We proceeded to drive back through the tunnel and entered the circular parking area. I turned the car around and parked in front of the granite monolith we had almost run into. I said, 'In the morning we will be bringing seven of our friends to this place. We should just get out and ask if it would be all right to do this.' Devin agreed.

I shut the engine off, and we just sat there. All I remember saying was, "oooh." It was so dark we could not see our hands in front of our face. I turned on the dome light. 'This is as dark as any Inipi (sweat lodge) I have ever been in,' I said.

We knew it was necessary to get out and have this talk with the spirits of this place, so Devin and I stepped out and closed our doors. The car's dome light stayed on for about thirty seconds, as I made my way around to the passenger side next to Devin. When the dome light went out the darkness swallowed us up, to the point where the only thing visible was the starlight above us. Even with the starlight, we could not see each other or the giant granite monoliths that encircled us. We leaned back against the car and just looked up at the stars, mostly because they were the only things we could see at the time.

As we gazed up at the constellations, the Milky Way seemed brighter than I could remember. The stars began to multiply, and became brighter and brighter. They were becoming so numerous the spaces between them grew smaller. Before long, the entire area was lit up as though it were a full moon. The monoliths were all coming into view; the air was still and silent, not even the sound of a cricket. I have camped in the Colorado Mountains and even with that altitude, the stars were not as bright as they were this night in the Black Hills.

The energy in the area seemed to be rising rapidly with a crackling sound when Devin said he was beginning to feel sick and dizzy, and needed to get back into the car. He opened the door, sat down, and closed it behind him. I walked over to where the monolith Needle's Eye was located and began looking up at the stars when a voice said; *This is where we brought Black Elk.*

The statement did not make a lot of sense to me, as I knew members of Black Elk's family and had even read the book *Black Elk Speaks*. The idea spirits brought him to the Needle's Eye was foreign to me. Neither the family nor the book ever mentioned the Needle's Eye. As I stood in the darkness looking around, I noticed the circle of granite monoliths began to look more like large tepee poles with all the bright stars appearing to be the covers. I began to think about what a Medicine Man had said about the spirit world being a mirror of the natural world. When the spirits took Black Elk to the rainbow tepee, it was in the spirit world. I concluded the mirror of the rainbow tepee must be Needle's Eye. About two miles from Needle's Eye is Harney Peak; its mirror is the highest mountain of them all, which is also located within the spirit world.

One point I would like to make is, the circular parking lot and road sets on top of 25 to 30 feet of back-fill. If the parking lot, road, and back-fill were not here, then these granite monoliths would stand 60 to 70 feet tall as they did in Black Elk's time.

It was after 2:00 am. I wanted to spend the entire night in this sacred place but the trip back to our campsite would take at least 45 minutes to an hour, and we needed to leave to prepare the group for the return trip in the early morning. This time, I remembered to ask if it would be okay to bring our friends to this sacred place. What I heard was; *It is not for you to ask permission for anyone, if they want to come here, each person needs to ask for themselves.*

Remembering the Sparrow vision from last year, I said both Devin and I would be starting our Sun Dance in July, all I heard was; *We know.* I guess I was hoping for, 'good job, we are so proud of you two'.

When I entered the car, Devin said, "All I could do was sit with my chin in my chest and drool all over the front of my shirt. It was like they shut me down." I guess we get out of life what we can handle at the time; they (spirits) have their way of protecting us from an overload, or maybe it was their way of communicating with Devin. The trip back to our camp that evening only took about 25 minutes, then again, who's complaining.

Figure 8: This is the granite wall Devin and I almost drove into.

Figure 9: Viewed from the parking lot, looking east into Needle's Eye tunnel, this is what Devin and I thought was a cave and drove through following the goat

The following morning, our group departed in three cars for Needle's Eye. The trip would take us through Keystone, past Mount Rushmore on Route 244, to Highway 16 toward Custer, and Route 87 toward Sylvan

Lake. On Route 87, we came upon four switchbacks and then entered a narrow tunnel before reaching the Custer State Park Ranger Station located by Sylvan Lake.

We paid the entrance fee and within 15 minutes arrived at Needle's Eye. The entire trip took us about 45 minutes, which was odd as Devin's and my earlier drive took us only 25 minutes in the dark of night to reach our camp. The oddity was Devin and I did not encounter these four switchbacks, or the narrow tunnel either going to or coming from the Needle's Eye that evening. At the time, we thought we must have taken a different road in the dark, one that was not on our maps. It would be the summer of 2005 before I would have a better understanding of what this time-discrepancy was all about (more to come on this subject later).

In July 1996, Devin and I began our first Sun Dance. Steve McCullough was the sponsor who petitioned an Ogalala Lakota Medicine Man by the name of Vernal Cross Sr. to act as the intercessor for the Sun Dance. On the fourth day of purification (four days of sweat lodges), the dancers tied their sixty-foot-long ropes onto the upper trunk of a forty-foot tall cottonwood tree, stood it upright, and placed it into a six-foot-deep hole located in the center of the Sun Dance arbor. Vernal stood silently looking at the tree and then said, "There is a man sitting in the tree; this is a good sign, as the spirits approve of this dance."

On the last day of dance, Devin stood pierced to the tree in the north side of the arbor. I stood pierced to the tree on the south side, the same positions we were sitting one year earlier, in relation to our fire pit, when we received the sparrow vision to dance. As of this writing 2016, I have danced the Sun Dance for twenty-one years consecutively. Earl was correct, "If you dance with all the energy you have to give, the Sun Dance will keep you young and strong." When people ask, who told you to dance, I just say, 'a little bird told me.'

The following year Vernal addressed several us and said, "The reason he came to this Sun Dance was due to Black Elk's Great Vision." He went on to say, "This dance is like the great hoop of Black Elk's vision, it is made up of many hoops of his people, all colors throughout the world."

Chapter 11: The First Ascent Clarified

The following is a summary account from John G. Neihardt's *Black Elk Speaks*, Chapter 3 The Great Vision.

Black Elk:

The Great Spirit said; The nations hoop is sacred and has no end. Behold all the power within the people will be one power that has no end. Now your people will pack everything up and step onto the long red road with their grandfathers alongside them. Black Elk watched his people break down their camps and step onto the 'red road' keeping the white giants wing to their faces.

As they marched, they lined up in a long column starting first, the black horse troop holding the wooden cup of water; next the white horse troop holding the white giants wing and the herb of power. After these the sorrel horse troop, holding the sacred pipe of peace and behind them came the buckskin horse troop holding the blossoming red stick with young children behind them.

Second, the people's four chiefs came with their band of young men and women.

Third, the people's four advisers came with men and women, not young or old.

Fourth, the old men came with canes, bent over and staggering as they walked.

Behind them and fifth, were old women with their canes, bent over and staggering as they walked.

Black Elk was the sixth, riding the bay horse and holding the bow and arrow. He said when he looked to the rear of the column he saw ghosts of elders, generation upon generation strung-out like smoke, like trailing stars, they were more than could be counted.

Clarification:

The Great Mystery was telling Black Elk the sacred hoop of the people extends beyond the imagination, and the people's power should be one power. When the people are divided, their hoops are small, when the people come together, the hoop is without end.

The idea the people broke camp and took the 'good red road' suggests the people were walking in the Lakota spiritual way of life. The 'good red road' runs from where the Great White Giant lives, the north, through to where we are all facing the south, they knew the Six Grandfathers were walking with them and would be close by. The White Giant's Wing on their faces meant they would face life's challenges with courage and endurance. The order of their march represented the four divides of life: infancy, youth, middle age, and old age. When we look at the four divides of life with respect to the four directions, it becomes clearer in the following description.

We are born in the South; infancy and childhood, we then advance to the West where we find our power, youth, young men, and women. We then advance to the north where we find our white hairs, middle age, men and women who are not young or old. We then move around to the East where we find knowledge and wisdom, old age, men and women staggering with their canes. We then complete the cycle and return to the South where we find our second childhood, just before we pass into the spirit world. This concept of advancing through the aging process is an important way of life to the Lakota.

The Grandfathers used the four-horse troop to represent the four directions. Their order of marching was: first the black horse troop (the west) carried the wooden cup of water representing life; second the white horse troop, (the north) carried the white giant's wing creating endurance and courage, and the herb of power, the healing herb. Third the sorrel horse troop (the east) carried the sacred pipe of peace, and fourth the buckskin horse troop (the south) carried the blossoming red stick, and the hoop of the nation. Behind the buckskin horse troop came the young children. These represented the four directions and all carried the gifts Black Elk gave the people.

They also used six groups to represent the six directions: Grandfather of the West, the North, the East, the South, Great Mystery the up, and Grandfather Earth the down. The four-horse troop with the children represent the "First" group

"Second" (the north) were the people's four chiefs with young men and women (youth). "Third" (the east) were the people's four advisers with men and women not young or old (middle age). The four advisers were select people that organized the moving of the camp, and or the hunt. "Fourth" (the south) were the old men with their canes staggering (old age) "Fifth" (the up) were the old women with their canes staggering (old age). "Sixth" (the down) was Black Elk himself with the bow and arrow that represented the power to destroy. These all represented the six directions.

Black Elk:

As the people took the 'good red road,' a voice proclaimed the people were walking in a sacred way on pleasant ground.

When Black Elk looked ahead, he saw four ascents laying before him and he thought they might be generations he would experience. As the people began to walk upon the first ascent, Black Elk noticed the land all about him was green. As they walked, the elders held their hands up with their palms facing outward and together they chanted quietly as clouds took on the shapes of infant faces.

When the people reached the summit of the first ascent, they setup their camp in a great hoop and at its center was the blossoming tree and all the land was green.

Clarification:

The idea that ascents represented generations is a little hard to follow with respect to the historical events the Lakota and the wasichu would experience over the next four generations. As I previously stated, spirits have a different view of time than we do. The use of generations makes more sense if we do not try to attach the typical 30 years to each generation. I believe we need to look at the steepness of each ascent.

The first ascent for the most part was not steep, lasting only 13 years for the people to reach its summit; which could account for the shorter duration of time associated with it. The first ascent took place around 1863, the year Black Elk was born, through 1876, when most of the Lakota bands were still nomadic and practiced the Lakota spiritual way of life.

The sky filled with clouds of infant faces suggests the people were traveling south on the 'good red road'. The infant faces represent children that are born in the south, and then advance through the four divides of life.

The following is a summary account from *Blue Water Creek and the first Sioux war 1854-1856*, by R. Eli Paul, 2004 Edition, University of Oklahoma Press.

On August 19, 1854, the first fight between the Sicangu Lakota (Brulé Sioux) and the US Government took place along the North Platt River in Nebraska. The Army initiated the fight over the killing of a Mormon cow by High Forehead, a Miniconju Lakota. Second Lieutenant Lawrence Grattan, his interpreter and twenty-nine enlisted men entered a Sicangu Lakota camp to arrest High Forehead for killing the cow. Conquering Bear, the head chief tried to reason with Grattan, asking him to wait for the Indian agent. Frustrated, Grattan ordered his soldiers to open fire on the village killing Conquering Bear. The Lakota warrior's rode down on Grattan and his command killing them all. September 3, 1855, General

Harney and six hundred cavalry and dragoons (infantrymen) attacked the Sicangu Lakota on the Blue Water Creek in Nebraska; causing heavy loses to the Lakota. This battle is known as the Blue Water Fight.

The Lakota had many fights with the US Government during this time in their history, without suffering any significant loss to the Lakota spiritual way of life, until their fight with General Custer and his seventh Cavalry in 1876.

Chapter 12: The Second Ascent Clarified

The following is a summary account from John G. Neihardt's *Black Elk Speaks*, Chapter 3, The Great Vision.

Black Elk:

As the people began the second ascent, they lined up as before, and the land all around them was green. Black Elk noticed as they walked, the road became steeper. When they were nearing the summit of the second ascent, the people changed into buffalo and all four-footed beings and even into winged ones, marching together on the 'good red road.' Black Elk himself was a spotted eagle floating high above them.

All the animals and fowls become apprehensive because they were not the same as before, crying out to their chiefs for guidance. When the people camped at the summit of the second ascent Black Elk noticed the leaves began falling from the sacred tree. As he stood there watching a voice said; *Observe your people and think about what the Grandfathers have given you, from this day forth the people will struggle on their journey.* "

Clarification:

The second ascent was getting a little steeper, taking the people a little longer to reach its summit. This ascent lasted about 15 years, starting around 1876 through 1891. The Lakota were trying to hold onto their spiritual ways despite the US Government's policy of forcing them onto reservations. As they drew close to the end of the second ascent, the people were still marching as before along the 'good red road.' They then changed into four-footed beings and even into fowls. This implies that rabbits, mice, coyotes or fowl are not compatible allies. As the Lakota camped at the summit of the second ascent, they began to disagree with each other on how to proceed with the US Government and even on how to follow their spiritual way of life.

The following is a summary account from *The Lance and the Shield-The Life and Times of Sitting Bull*, by Robert M. Utley, 1994 Edition First Ballantine Books, Chapters 11, 12 and 13, pages 131-167. It tells of what the people were going through during the second ascent.

Clarification:

On June 4, 1876, Sitting Bull (a Hunkpapa Lakota Medicine Man) organized a Sun Dance to fulfill a vow he made at the end of May, while praying to the Great Mystery about the plight of the Lakota with respect to the white man. During the Sun Dance, Sitting Bull had fifty pieces of flesh taken from his left arm and then had fifty pieces taken from his right arm, totaling one hundred pieces of flesh. After many hours of dancing and gazing at the sun, he stopped in a trance-like state. When he came out of the trance, he said the spirits gave him a vision of soldiers and horses riding down on the Lakota village. As they came, they were upside down, their hats falling off as the soldiers and horses fell into camp. In this vision, Sitting Bull said, "The soldiers would die and some Indians would die." He repeated what the voice said; *These soldiers do not have ears, they will die and you are not supposed to pillage their bodies.*

On June 17, 1876, around 500 Lakota and Cheyenne warriors led by Crazy Horse (an Oglala Lakota) and Sitting Bull, fought the battle of the Rosebud, routing General Crook's forces that were twice as large as the Indian's. Due to the lack of supplies and wounded soldiers, Crook decided to return to his base camp at the head of the Tongue River to re-group. What is important is, this attack by the Lakota and Cheyenne, unnerved Crook to the point he would not re-enter the Indian campaign until he could reinforce his troops. It would be six weeks before he was prepared to move his troops back into the field, counting his forces out of the up and coming events between the Indians and General Custer's Seventh Calvary. On June 18, after the battle of the Rosebud the Lakota moved to the Greasy Grass of Montana.

Sitting Bull said he did not think the fight at the Rosebud connected with his vision of soldier's upside down. He felt this fight was going to happen soon, as the soldiers in his vision were attacking a Lakota village. In a span of six days, the village grew from 450 lodges (with about 3,000 Indians) to 1,000 lodges (with over 7,000 Indians), having about 1,800 warriors.

On June 24, due to the size of their camp the Lakota moved eight miles down the river to the Greasy Grass, along the Little Bighorn River. The village was three miles long and almost a mile thick in places. Due to the large size of the Cheyenne, they protected the village in the north end, and the Brulé, Oglala, Sans Arc, Miniconju, and Blackfoot were in the middle, with the Hunkpapa protecting the south end of the village.

On June 25, 1876, General Custer and 750 men of the Seventh Cavalry positioned themselves to attack the Lakota village. Custer made the decision to split his forces into three groups. He sent Captain Frederick W. Benteen with one battalion to scout south along the foot of the Wolf Mountains for signs of Indian activity. He then ordered Major Marcus A. Reno with one battalion of 175 men, including a tracker named Bloody Knife and fifteen Ree scouts, to attack the Lakota village from the southwest. Custer would move the remaining battalion of around 210 men to the northeast, with the intent of cutting off the fleeing Indians, as Reno attacked their camp from the southwest. Benteen's battalion would bring up the rear with the mule train and one company as escort.

Custer did not count on over 1,800 hardened Lakota and Cheyenne warriors bring the fight to the famous Seventh Cavalry. In the span of a short time, the warriors routed Reno and his command driving them out of the village and onto the high bluffs east of the Little Bighorn River. Of

175 men, 40 men died, 13 were wounded and 16 were left behind in the thickets below (they too would eventually meet their end at the hands of the Lakota warriors).

As the fighting was erupting in the south end of the village, Custer drove his battalion down the steep bluffs toward the river in the north end of the village. At Medicine Tail Coulee, Custer stationed three companies on the North Slope to hold that position. He sent two companies down Medicine Tail to frighten the Indians and hold their retreat. Much to his surprise, the Indians were not running away; they were running at him. After a short fight, the two companies retreated and headed northeast for the high ground. Custer and the remaining three companies moved north in hopes of a reunion of all five companies, only to find the Lakota and Cheyenne warriors waiting for them. When the fighting was over, Custer and his battalion of 210 men lay dead and 53 men of Reno's command killed in the valley and on the bluffs, with 60 men wounded.

After Benteen joined Reno, their combined forces numbered 350 men of the surviving Seventh Cavalry. A halfhearted attempt by a detachment led by Benteen moved north to help Custer. What they encountered was returning Indians from the Custer fight. They had to fight their way back to their original position on the hill with Reno's command. As night approached, both Reno and Benteen's men dug throughout the night, a large elliptical hole for protection.

When the battle with Custer and his men was over, the women and warriors alike stripped the soldiers of their clothing and possessions, and in some cases butchered and maimed the dead. Due to their hate and anger at what these soldiers had done by attacking their village, the Lakota had gone against the voice of Sitting Bull's vision of soldiers falling into the village. The voice said; *These soldiers do not have ears, they will die and you are not supposed to pillage their bodies.*

This single event was the greatest battle the Lakota would ever fight; it would also be the deciding blow, which would begin to strip away the Lakota spiritual way of life.

Sitting Bull felt his people went against the vision of his Sun Dance by robbing the bodies of the soldiers. One Bull told the people what Sitting Bull had told him: the people should not desire the things of the white man or it will be their curse. Later Sitting Bull told his people, "For your failure to obey my vision, from this time forth you shall always want the white man's possessions."

The many church groups supporting the Lakota would begin to unravel after the killing and butchering of Custer's Seventh Cavalry, allowing the US Government to withhold funds and rations, until some of the Lakota agreed to give up the Black Hills and the unseeded territory bound by the treaty of 1868.

The following is a summary account from John G. Neihardt's *Black Elk Speaks*, Chapter 12 Grandmothers Land.

Clarification:

On May 6, 1877, Crazy Horse and 889 of his people arrived at Fort Robinson, Nebraska and surrendered. In early May, Sitting Bull and about 15 lodges crossed into Canada and joined some 3,500 Lakota who had already settled in Grandmother's land (Queen of England). On September 5, 1877, a soldier killed Crazy Horse when he resisted arrest on trumped up charges. As hard as this was for the Lakota, their impression that the land was still green meant their spiritual path was still rooted on the 'good red road.' In 1878, Black Elk and a small band of Lakota headed for Canada to join up with Sitting Bull and Galls people in an attempt to hold onto their Lakota spiritual way of Life, all of this was happening during the second ascent, and would set the stage for Black Elk's statement:

[The people changed into buffalo and all four-footed beings and even into winged ones, marching together on the 'good red road.' I turned into a spotted eagle floating high above them. As we were nearing the summit of the second ascent, all the animals and fowl become apprehensive that they were not the same as before, crying out to their chiefs for guidance.]

The following is a summary account of what Black Elk was experiencing during the second ascent, from age 13 through 28. from John G. Neihardt's *Black Elk Speaks*, Chapter 12 through 20.

Clarification:

Black Elk spoke about the Hang-Around-The-Fort-People with some disappointment, but with a fair assessment, these Lakota wanted peace while maintaining their spiritual way of life, despite living so close to the wasichu. The fighting was never over land where the Lakota were concerned; it was about losing their sacred Black Hills and hunting grounds. The Hunkpapa Lakota would not encroach on Oglala Lakota hunting grounds without asking permission. All the Plains Indian tribes understood and respected this; the wasichu did not.

In the late fall of 1879, Black Elk, his father, mother and a small band of his people returned to their homeland in South Dakota. In spring of 1880, at age seventeen, Black Elk told an old Medicine Man by the name of Black Road about his vision of the flowering tree. Black Road instructed him to perform the Horse Dance to bring his vision to the people. With Black Road's help, he performed the horse dance.

At age eighteen, he made his first vision quest and shortly afterwards performed the Dog Vision. In 1882, at age nineteen, he performed his first healing ceremony and the buffalo ceremony. In 1883, at age twenty, he performed the elk ceremony. Black Elk performed all these ceremonies to reenact the great vision for his people.

By 1883, the wasichu, for no more than their hides or tongues, slaughtered the last of the buffalo herds. The US Government denies the slaughter of the buffalo was done to starve the Lakota and force them onto the reservations. I believe our history speaks for itself: all the US Government had to do was look the other way allowing the wasichu to hunt the buffalo into extinction. Once the buffalo were gone, the Lakota had no choice but to become dependent on the US Government and move onto the reservations. Afterwards, the US Government began withholding the promised provisions of food, clothing, etc., until the Lakota agreed to sign new treaties, surrendering even more land.

In 1886, when Black Elk was twenty-three years old, he joined Buffalo Bill's Wild West show, traveling to New York and then to England to understand how the wasichu lived. He thought about his vision and the daybreak-star herb, the herb of understanding. If he could understand how the wasichu lived, then maybe it would help him to bring the sacred hoop of the people back and make the tree bloom again. He traveled around England experiencing the wasichu hospitality, as these people were not trying to kill him or take his people's land.

When Black Elk joined Mexican Joe's show, he spent some time in London, and then went on to Paris where he met a young girl, whose parents liked him. When Black Elk became sick, he stayed with the girl's parents who helped cure him. During his stay, Black Elk had a vision, an out of body experience, where he traveled back to Pine Ridge on a little cloud and looked down on his people and his mother. When she looked up at the cloud, it reversed course and took Black Elk back to the home in Paris. When Black Elk opened his eyes, the girl's family was frightened, telling him he looked dead for three days, taking only small breaths occasionally. A few days later Black Elk reconnected with Buffalo Bill who arranged to send him back to his home on the Pine Ridge Reservation.

The following is a summary account from *The Ghost-Dance Religion and The Sioux Outbreak of 1890* by James Mooney, 1991 Edition First Bison Book, Chapter 8 and 9, pages 746-776.

Clarification:

In 1881, a religion known as the "Shakers" originated with the tribes of Puget Sound, Washington. A young man by the name of Wovoka (Jack Wilson) learned the hypnotic secrets from these tribes and applied some of their traditions to a vision given to him around January 1, 1889. During a total eclipse of the sun, Wovoka fell into a deep trance and there he saw God and all the people who had died long ago. All the people were young and happy, with an abundance of game.

Early in the spring of 1889, a delegation of Lakota consisting of Good Thunder and several others traveled west to meet the "Messiah" (Wovoka). When the delegation returned to the Lakota, they described Wovoka as the Indian messiah, the son of God. They went on to say, Wovoka wanted the people to dance to bring back the Indian way of life and they should not tell the white man he is here. They are not to tell lies, refuse to work or fight with the white man. They must dance 4 nights and one day to bring back the Indian way of life. The white man and all Indian people who worked with the white man will disappear. All their dead relatives would come back to life and the buffalo would return to the Plains.

In 1890, a second delegation consisting of Good Thunder, Cloud Horse, Yellow Knife, and Short Bull returned to meet with the Messiah, and upon their return to Pine Ridge confirmed the earlier findings. In the spring of 1890, the inauguration of the Ghost Dance began at the Pine Ridge.

The following is a summary account from John G. Neihardt's *Black Elk Speaks*, Chapter 21 The Messiah.

Clarification:

Black Elk returned to his people in the summer of 1889, only to find the Lakota in despair; rations and supplies had been cut, and sickness was everywhere. His father died that year from the sickness.

The first reports of the Ghost Dance came to the Lakota and everyone was excited. By 1890, many Lakota were doing the Ghost Dance throughout the reservations. Black Elk began to see the correlation between the Ghost Dance and his Great Vision of the sacred hoop and blossoming tree. Before long Black Elk immersed himself into the Ghost Dance, hopeful in that it will help bring about the blossoming tree of his great vision.

In December 1890, the Standing Rock Indian agent James McLaughlin sent the Indian police to arrest Sitting Bull for helping to organize the Ghost Dance. When he resisted, the Indian police killed him. This was extremely odd, as Sitting Bull did not associate or direct the Ghost Dance. He did however help decipher some of the visions people were having.

Black Elk was now twenty-seven years old and on December 29, 1890, soldiers from Custer's old seventh Cavalry surrounded Spotted Elk's (Big Foot) band at Wounded Knee Creek, South Dakota. They consisted of about 350 Miniconju and some Hunkpapa Lakota fleeing from Sitting Bull's camp after the police had killed him. There were about 120 warriors, with the rest of the camp consisting of women, children, and elders. The soldiers were disarming the warriors when a shot rang out. Then all hell broke loose. The soldiers opened fire on the entire camp, killing any-thing that moved. They were mostly unarmed warriors, women, children, and elders, and even some of their own soldiers. By the end of the day, nearly two hundred Lakota men, women, and children died.

Due to the mistrust and hardship the Lakota had suffered under the control of the US Government, they embraced the Ghost Dance with the notion all the dead relatives and buffalo would return.

Chapter 13: The Third Ascent Clarified

Now, the people would step off the 'good red road,' the road of high spirituality, and begin the walk of the 'black road', the road of hardship and war. For the next two ascents, the people would walk the 'black road', as predicted in Black Elk's vision.

The following is a summary account from John G. Neihardt's *Black Elk Speaks*, Chapter 3 The Great Vision.

Black Elk:
When the people were ready to start the third ascent, they saw the 'black road' ahead. The 'black road' goes from where the thunder beings live in the west, through to where the sun shines always, the east, a fearful road of hardship and war. As they walked the 'black road', they saw black storm clouds coming on them fast and did not want to leave but they could not remain. The people were still four-footed animals and every bird that was, and they ran in all directions seeking their own visions and making up their own little rules to follow. Throughout the universe, Black Elk could hear the winds of battle and the sound of screaming creatures fighting everywhere.

When the people camped at the summit of the third ascent, Black Elk saw that the hoop of the people was broken like smoke from a fire, dispersing in all directions. The blossoming tree was dying; the leaves and birds were gone, and when Black Elk looked, he saw the fourth ascent and said it would be dreadful.

Clarification:

The third ascent was much steeper than the first and second ascents, taking 48 years for the people to reach its summit, starting from 1891 through around 1939.

The following is a summary account from the Native American Rights Fund, Justice Newsletter Winter 1997.

In the 1890's, the US Government successfully stopped the Ghost Dance throughout the United States and by 1904, the Government had banned the Sun Dance and other ceremonies they believed to be Indian offenses. If the Lakota violated these laws, the Government withheld rations or even imprisoned them. It was also illegal to be in possession of sacred items like eagle feathers, eagle parts, etc. The ban on ceremonies would remain in force until 1934, but continued to ban Lakota men from piercing to the tree during the Sun Dance.

In 1978, the American Indian Religious Freedom Act lifted the ban on men piercing to the tree and possessing sacred items such as hawk, eagle feathers, or eagle parts. The ban on possessing hawk, eagle feathers or parts, still exists for non-Indian people.

Clarification:

With prohibition of sacred ceremonies, it is no wonder the Lakota suffered during the third ascent. Many Lakota began looking to Christianity for their spiritual needs. The notion a Lakota person could move from the Lakota sacred way of life into the Christian concept was not hard to fathom. The Lakota way of life was not so different from Christian teachings, with one important exception: the Lakota way of life is earth based.

What is difficult for many people to understand with respect to the US Government's prohibition on sacred ceremonies is how could a country, founded on religious freedom, ever outlaw the American Indians right to practice their spiritual way of life.

Speaking of Christianity, what the wasichu were going through during the last two ascents were: fear, hate, jealousy, prejudice, and greed, just a few tools of the negative force. During this time in history, the wasichu were deeply involved in its use.

US Government used the concept of Manifest Destiny to expand US territories, portraying the American Indian as being inferior and a savage, thereby replacing darkness with light and ignorance with civilization.

The wasichu were not acting as good Christians when they raided villages, arbitrarily killing women, children, and elders. They took what they wanted and then left the rest, if it had no value. The US Government made treaties with the Lakota and other tribes, and then later broke the treaty if something of value appeared, such as gold in the Black Hills of South Dakota.

These were dark times for the United States and its citizen. They would suffer as much spiritual loss as the Lakota, if not more. The Lakota did not willingly walk away from their spiritual way of life. In many cases, the hardened traditional Lakota simply took these sacred ceremonies underground, away from the watchful eyes of the Christianized Lakota and Indian agents in charge of the reservations, preserving the culture, language and ceremonial practices for the next generation.

The following is a summary account from necrometrics.com, John Ellis & Michael Cox, the World War I, 1914 - 1918 Datebook.

In 1914 through 1918, World War I dragged the world into chaos, creating many atrocities perpetrated on humankind by way of ethnic cleansing and other careless acts of cruelty. Approximately 8.5 million military and 6.5 million civilians died in this short period.

The People's Hoop was broken and the blossoming tree was dying. In 1932, when John G Neihardt was interviewing Black Elk for the book *Black Elk Speaks*, Black Elk said they were close to the end of the third ascent and soon, something horrible was going to happen throughout the world.

Chapter 14: The Fourth Ascent Clarified

Black Elk:

As the people were preparing to begin the fourth ascent Black Elk heard a voice say; look at your people, and when he looked down he saw his people had changed back into humans. Their ribs stood out for they were puny and sick, their horses were starving, and the blossoming tree was dead.

Clarification:

The fourth ascent would be extremely steep compared to the third ascent; taking place around 1939, through the present time of this writing, 2016, as my generation makes up the fourth ascent. When the people began the fourth ascent, the starvation represented the people's loss of their spiritual connection to their sacred way of life. The buffalo and the blossoming tree were gone, reinforcing their dependence on the US Government for survival.

The following is a summary account from John G. Neihardt's *Black Elk Speaks*, Chapter 3 The Great Vision.

Black Elk:

As Black Elk stood looking at his people, he cried and then noticed a man painted red, standing in the north of the camp. The man walked to the center of the camp holding a spear, there he lay down, rolled over and stood up, and was a big buffalo standing in the center of the camp. Where the buffalo was standing, an herb began to grow in the precise spot the blossoming tree had been. This herb had a single stem, with four blossoms: a blue, white, scarlet and yellow, and the light from these lit up the sky.

Black Elk said he knew what this meant; the buffalo was the people's strength and a gift from the Great Mystery. They would lose the buffalo and must find new strength from the four-blossoming herb. The people and their horses were happier when the herb had blossomed, and, as he stood there, he saw a light wind blowing from the north amongst the people. Abruptly the blossoming tree was there again at the center of the nation, in the place the herb had grown and bloomed.

Clarification:

The man painted red represents the sacred color of purity, strength, and endurance; the spear represents the hunter/warrior. The buffalo was like a Big Wal-Mart store, everything they needed came from the buffalo: food, clothing, utensils and shelter. It supported their independence, and sacred way of life. The sacred herb that replaced the buffalo would become the people's new strength. Black Elk said this herb bore four blossoms on a single stem: a blue, a white, a scarlet and a yellow. Blue can also represent the color black, the power of the west.

When Black Elk gave the vision of the flowering tree to John G. Neihardt, Black Elk represented the man painted red all over. He was standing at the center of the nation's hoop, calling the four directions to its center: black, red, yellow, and white.

Again, the four-blossoming herb contained the same colors of the four main races of humankind: black, red, yellow, and white, coming together from the four directions, to the center of the nation's hoop.

Black Elk:

Black Elk was still the spotted eagle soaring over his people and realized he was entering the fourth ascent. The land was dark and terrifying all around him, the winds of the earth were doing battle. It sounded like swift gunfire, like swirling dust, and like people sobbing and ear-piercing cries of horses throughout the world.

His people ran here and there strapping down their tepees against the high winds as black storm clouds fell upon them, with terrified swallows taking flight before the storm.

Clarification:

From the height of the spotted eagle, Black Elk knew the fourth ascent would be horrifying for the people of the world. When Black Elk spoke of all the winds of the earth fighting, he was referring to the people of four directions of the earth and the coming of hardship and war. He saw his people struggling against the force of the four winds of the earth, desperately trying to hold onto what little hope they had left.

The following paragraphs reference only approximate number of deaths from the wars that occurred throughout the world since 1939, to the present time of this writing.

The following is a summary account from necrometrics.com, Messenger, the Chronological Atlas (1989) of World War II, 1939 -1945.

The people had already gone through the World War I, and by 1937, Japan would invade China. From 1939, through 1945, the world experiences World War II. The atrocities of World War I would seem pale next to what would happen during the period of the fourth ascent. Approximately 22 million military and 28 million civilians would perish in this short war.

The following is a summary account from necrometrics.com, COWP: Correlates of War Project at the University of Michigan, Korea conflict, 1950 - 1953.

In 1950, the world would find itself in the Korean Conflict, a nice way of avoiding the word, war. This war lasted from 1950 through 1953, with approximately 1.8 million military and 1.6 million civilians would perish in this short war.

The following is a summary account from necrometrics.com, Twentieth Century Atlas - Death Tolls; Vietnam conflict, 1965 - 1975.

The next conflict would take place in Vietnam from 1965 through 1975. The US began sending military advisers as early as 1960, and by 1965, they began sending combat units to the field. Estimations are 943,605 military and 365,000 civilians would perish in this war. There were about 65,000 North Vietnam civilians killed by US bombing in the north.

The following is a summary account from necrometrics.com, Twentieth Century Atlas - Death Tolls; Persian Gulf war, 1990 - 1991.

In 1990 through 1991, the world would find itself involved in the Persian Gulf War. This war was a result of Iraq invading Kuwait, which would prove to be a shortened war. The United Nations (UN), led by the United States, forced Saddam Hussein's Iraqi military out of Kuwait. Approximately 25,185 military and 7,375 civilians would perish in this short war.

The following is a summary account from necrometrics.com, Twentieth Century Atlas - Death Tolls, Bosnian War, 1992- 1995.

In April 1992 through December 1995, the UN would get involved in the Bosnian War. The Bosnian Serbs, supported by the Serbian government of Slobodan Milosevic and the Yugoslav People's Army (JNA), attacked the Republic of Bosnia and Herzegovina; mainly Muslim Bosnians. Muslim Bosnian losses were approximately 60,000 military and

160,000 civilian. Most civilian losses were the product of ethnic cleansing and careless acts of cruelty. The Serb and Croatia losses were about 25,000 to 60,000 military and 4,700 civilian. After the war, 45 Serbs, 12 Croats and 4 Bosnians were convicted of war crimes.

The following is a summary account from necrometrics.com, Twentieth Century Atlas Death Tolls; September 11, 2001 Attack of World Trade Center.

On September 11, 2001, members of the terrorist group "Al-Qaeda," hijacked four passenger planes, and flew two of them into the World Trade Center, located in New York City, one into the Pentagon and one plane crashed into a field in Shanks Ville Pennsylvania, (caused by some of passengers trying to take back control of the aircraft). On this day 3,018 men, women and children would perish through this act of insanity, and Al-Qaeda terrorist losses were 19.

On October 7, 2001, to the present day 2014, the US and members of the United Nations began a bombing campaign in Afghanistan to strike at Al-Qaeda and the Taliban. As of 2011, estimations are over 32,847 military and 14,700 civilians would perish in this long war.

The following is a summary account from necrometrics.com, Twentieth Century Atlas - Death Tolls; Iraq War 2003 - 2011.

On March 20, 2003, through 2011, The US and its allies began the invasion of Iraq, due to the suspicion of Iraq holding weapons of mass destruction (WMD). The notion Saddam Hussein refused the United Nations inspections set the entire invasion in motion, as they could not confirm as to whether Iraq was in possession of WMD. Right or wrong, this war would cost US and Allied forces about 16,400 deaths; Al-Qaeda and Iraqi Insurgents would suffer losses of about 19,000. The total civilian deaths were at about 126,000, the majority caused by Al-Qaeda and Iraqi Insurgent acts of terrorism.

Clarification:

The need to list the past wars the world engaged in during the fourth ascent is indicative of the darkness associated with the 'black road', and the struggle the people of the world will endure. In World War II, 28 million civilians died in the short span of six years. In the ten-year war in Afghanistan, 14,700 civilians died. When we compare, the deaths caused by these wars, it becomes evident the US and Europe began to avoid civilian casualties, as a matter of conscience and the principal of winning the hearts and minds of the people.

Today, when the United States or Allied personnel kill civilians deliberately, they are charged with murder. A far cry from the days of the Wounded Knee Massacre of 1890, when members of Custer's old 7th Cavalry rode their horses along the dry gulch and killed Lakota men, women, and children.

Today, with respect to all the wars the people have endured and are still involved in during the fourth ascent, this represents the change of heart. The killing of unarmed men, women, and children has become intolerable behavior throughout the entire world, with exception of a few groups. As we draw close to the end of the fourth ascent, people will begin to find the light. You might have noticed I have begun using the term "people," instead of wasichu, more to come on the term, "the people."

The following is a summary account from John G. Neihardt's *Black Elk Speaks*, Chapter 3 The Great Vision,

Black Elk:

As Black Elk stood in the dark grasp of the fourth ascent, a song came to him and was like this:

A nation that is good, I will give life.

This the spirits above have said.

The spirits have given me the power to restore.

After Black Elk sang the song a voice said; *Run to the four directions and cry for help, for nothing will be able to stop you.*

Clarification:

In Black Elk's song, he states that he will heal the people's spirit, which the Six Grandfathers have said and he will have the power to reverse the negative and bring the flowering tree back to life, 'to make over.'

The concept of running to the four directions for help suggests Black Elk will bring all the people from the four directions to the center of the nation's hoop and then nothing will be able to stop him and the people from bringing the flowering tree back to life.

Black Elk:

Black Elk and his bay horse were back on earth, because the horse and Black Elk are of the earth, as the earth is where he will find his power. There he saw a faded black horse, puny and sick standing in the west. He heard a voice say; *Take this herb and remake him.* Black Elk looked down and saw he was holding the four-blossoming herb, so he rode around the sick horse in a circle while people far-off called for spirit. The sick horse rolled, whinnied and stood up and was a beautiful black stallion standing there. His mane flowed like a cloud, he snorted lightning, and his eyes glowed like the evening star, for he was the chief of all the horses.

Clarification:

The Grandfathers were repeating the lesson given to Black Elk in his earlier encounter with them to show him how to perform the doctoring on earth. Again, the four-blossoming herb with four blossoms on a single stem: blue, white, scarlet and yellow, represent the same colors of the four directions and of humankind. The voice told Black Elk how to use the four-blossoming herb of power to reverse the negative, and to make the black stallion over. Again, the black horse represented the First Grandfather, he of the West, and the thunder beings. The evening star is Venus; it is also the morning star. The stallion's sickness represented the spiritual starvation and dependency on alcohol and drugs, a struggle many of the people today endure.

Black Elk:

The black stallion raced toward the west and called out. The sky filled with shiny black horses plummeting from the clouds. He turned toward the north and called out. The sky filled with white horses without number, diving and turning as they came. Then he turned to the east and the south. Once again, the sky filled with horses without number, sorrels and buckskins, plummeting toward the earth as they came. The four colors of horses came with joyfulness of their speed and power. Black Elk felt it was wonderful and terrifying at the same time.

Clarification:

When the black horse dashed to the west and neighed, the west filled with, shiny black horses more than could be counted. Then he dashed to the north and then to the east, and then to the south, calling the whites, the sorrels and the buckskins. The Grandfathers were showing Black Elk how to call upon the four directions for help. The horses were also representing the thunder beings that protect the people's sacred way of life from all negative energy. When spirit is working, it can be exciting and frightening at the same time.

Black Elk:

All the horses gathered in their quarters around the black stallion, which stood at the center of the nation's hoop. Then four stunning women (virgins) entered the circle from each of the four directions, wearing scarlet dresses and stood around the black stallion in their quarters. The woman from the west held the wooden cup of water, the woman from the north held the white wing, the woman from the east held the pipe, and the woman from the south held the hoop of the people.

Clarification:

The black horses, too many to count, stood in the west and the white, sorrel and buckskin horses all stood in their respective positions in the north, east and south. They encircled their black chief, the spirit of the West along with the thunder beings stood at the center of the nation's hoop. The horses represented the four directions, the west, north, east, and south, and the four colors of humankind, coming together in a circle around their chief. In retrospect, it is important to remember the black stallion is representative of the First Grandfather and said that he was Black Elk's spirit and that Black Elk was his body. Then, he gave him his name, 'Eagle Wing Stretches.' The Black Stallion was showing Black Elk how to stand at the center of the nation's hoop to be recognized and valued as a powerful Wicasa Wakáŋ.

The four virgins dressed in scarlet, coming through each of the four quarters represent purity, as both virgins (women) and the color red are symbolic with respect to purity. This suggests the four women purified each of the four directions, and each of the sacred gifts, the wooden cup of water (life), the white wing (endurance), the pipe (peace and healing), and the nation's hoop (the sacred circle). The bow and arrow stayed with Black Elk representing fear and destruction, something the women would not touch or try to purify.

Black Elk:

As the universe sat in silence, the black stallion sang a song. His song was not loud but it traveled throughout the universe. Everything everywhere heard the song and was more pleasing than songs can be. The song was so wonderful everything danced, the four virgins, the trees, and hills, rivers, four-legged, two-legged, and the winged ones all danced to the stallion's song.

Clarification:

Most people I have spoken with think "Mitakúye Oyasin" only means being a relative to each other, and they miss the point of being a relative to all things. In this statement, Black Elk witnessed the relationship with the trees, hills, the waters in the creeks and lakes, the four-legged, two-legged and the wings of the air all dancing together. Mitakúye Oyasin is the cornerstone of Black Elk's great vision, a relationship with all things.

Black Elk:

When Black Elk looked down upon his people, he saw a cloud pass over, dropping gentle rain and then stop in the east as a rainbow arched over it.

After this, the horses all returned to their places, singing with everything that had a voice, past the crest of the fourth ascent. He heard a voice say; *Throughout the universe, they finished a joyful day* and when he looked down, he saw the entire day spread out like a circle, pleasant and green, with all things growing, gentle and content.

Clarification:

Black Elk states when he looked down he saw his people and after the gentle rain, all the horses were singing and all things walked with them back to their places within the four directions and beyond the crest of the fourth ascent: the four-legged, winged, trees, rivers and lakes. This statement should help bolster the fact that Black Elk is being shown all the things in the universe are his people, Mitakúye Oyasin. One other point worth making in Black Elk's statement beyond the crest of fourth ascent is that this represents a promise of better things to come when we complete the fourth ascent.

Black Elk:

The voice told Black Elk this day was his to make and they will be taking him to stand at the center of the world to see.

As Black Elk rode east, upon his bay he knew the four-horse troop was behind him, starting with the west, next the north, then the east and last the south. He looked and saw the mountains and forests, and from these flashed every color towards the sky. When he arrived, he was standing in the mountains on the highest point and below him was the entire hoop of the earth. As he stood there, he was seeing all things and shapes as spirit saw them. It was more than he could express and he comprehended much more than he saw. Black Elk was seeing things as spirit saw them, a symbiotic relationship with all things, as they must live together as one.

Black Elk stood on the highest mountain of them all and looked down, and saw the hoop of the nation, which was made of many hoops of his people spreading out wide as the day and starlight, and at its center, was the blossoming tree to shade all children of one father and mother, and he knew it was sacred.

Clarification:

The location of the highest mountain of them all is Harney Peak, located in the Black Hills of South Dakota. Black Elk saw the whole hoop of the world as a place where all things must live together as one. The sacred hoop consisted of different cultural and religious practices of all his people. We are not just black, white, red, or yellow people, we are One. We are struggling together to find meaning. We are eight-legged, six-legged, four-legged, and two-legged, the winged, the swimmers, and the rooted ones: all things coming together to create many hoops of one circle, wide as the day and starlight.

This last paragraph suggests the Great Mystery knows the people will learn to respect and embrace each other, with respect to their religious and cultural differences, creating connecting circles to make one circle all around the earth wide as day and as starlight. Black Elk's vision indicates we must work together to create this sacred hoop and end the prejudice and misunderstandings that have divided us.

The two-legged (humans) utilize many religious practices or doctrines: Buddhist, Jewish, Christianity, Hindu, Muslim and the Lakota spiritual way of life, to name a few. What is important to understand is there is but one 'God,' with many different languages to pronounce the word. The Lakota have two ways to pronounce the name of God: Wakáŋ Táŋka Tunkasila, and Até Wakáŋ Táŋka (Father Great Mystery). Uncí Maká, (Grandmother Earth) Maká Iná (Mother Earth). The point in all this is, as Black Elk states, the blossoming tree would shelter all the children of 'one father and one mother' (Father Great Mystery and Mother Earth).

The blossoming tree at the center of the mighty circle of his people symbolizes the seventh direction, which is located at the center of the six directions and the universe. All things are located at the center, the dwelling place of the Great Mystery.

Chapter 15: The Daybreak Star

The following is a summary account from John G. Neihardt's *Black Elk Speaks*, Chapter 3, The Great Vision, [University of Nebraska Press, The Complete Edition, 2014.]

Black Elk:

Black Elk stood watching, as two men came from the east, flying like arrows. As they came, the Morning Star rose between them slowly. They presented him with the Morning Star herb of understanding and said; With this; whatever you do on earth, you will be successful. He was told to drop the herb onto the earth, and where it hit the ground it set forth roots and grew, four flowers on a single stem, a blue, white, scarlet and yellow. From these, beams of light streaked upward to the sky, and nowhere was it dark.

Clarification:

The two men were spirits of light. The Lakota believe all things have a spirit attached: light, air, water, trees, rocks, and two-legged to name a few. The Morning Star from the east brings the light of understanding and wisdom. Only in darkness will one find ignorance and misunderstanding. The herb of understanding: blue, (black) white, scarlet, and yellow blossoms represent the four directions and four main colors of humankind. Through the herb of understanding, Black Elk will bring the people, all the people, back to the 'good red road' throughout the four directions, replacing darkness (ignorance and misunderstanding) with light (understanding and wisdom).

Black Elk:

Then the voice told Black Elk he was to return to the Six Grandfathers. He noticed his body was painted all red, with black joints and stripes of white between them. Lightning bolts were all over his bay horse while his mane flowed like a cloud and lightning was Black Elk's breath.

Clarification:

Black Elk was to return to the Six Grandfathers for counsel, but before he made his journey, the spirits presented him with the powers of the west and north. The sacred color red represents purity and endurance, whereas black and white together represent Heyóka colors, the thunder Beings. Black Elk would be working with the thunder Beings of the west, the white giant's wing of the north, and would possess the powers of the Heyóka and the Wicasa Wakáŋ.

Black Elk:

The two men that first brought Black Elk to meet with the Grandfathers now escorted him on his return trip. As he followed them on his bay horse, they turned into four flocks of geese, flying in circles above each of the four directions, and as they flew, they cried out in their sacred voices.

Clarification:

The two men represent the thunder beings who originally accompanied Black Elk when he met with the Six Grandfathers at the rainbow tepee. The four circles of geese represent prayers rising from each of the four directions. The geese also represent all the people working together and praying through the four directions to send one prayer to Grandfather Great Mystery.

Black Elk:

As they drew near the place of the Six Grandfathers, Black Elk saw the rainbow tepee made of clouds and sewn with lightning. Beneath it the winged ones, and below them, all four-legged and two-legged - all happy. And the laughter was like thunder.

Clarification:

The rainbow tepee represented the heavens with birds flying below, then animals and humans walking together. Again, the rainbow tepee is in the spirit world, a mirror of the natural world; at this point Black Elk was seeing into both the spirit world and the natural world.

Black Elk:

As Black Elk rode through the door of the rainbow tepee, he saw the Six Grandfathers sitting in a line with their arms stretched out toward him. Behind them in the clouds, were faces of people without number, not yet born.

Clarification:

Dr. Gillihan explained that the Lakota believe that when a person makes their spirit journey (death), the Naġi stays around the area it enjoyed (like their home or a favorite park, etc.) for a short time. This is why some people state they can still feel a deceased person's energy around them. The To'wakaŋ, and the Niya', travel together up and along the Milky Way, taking four generations to arrive at heaven's gate. The ' To'wakaŋ enters heaven using their sacred name, and the Niya' travels to the north, recycles into the spirit pool, and waits to enter the open mouth of a newborn starting the whole process over again: birth, youth, middle age, old age and then death.

Black Elk:

The Six Grandfathers congratulated Black Elk for the journey he had completed and gave the same gifts they gave earlier: from the west came the wooden cup of water, and the bow and arrow, life and death. From the north, the White Giant's Wing brings endurance, and the herb of healing, from the east, the pipe of peace, and from the south, the blossoming red stick. As each of the Grandfathers spoke they explained what these gifts represented, and then each dissolved into the earth and then rose once again as the Grandfather standing there. After they did this, Black Elk felt closer to the earth.

Clarification:

The Lakota use a circular narrative in telling a story. For example, at the beginning of Black Elk's vision, he received gifts from the Grandfathers: a wooden cup of water, the bow and arrow, the white wing and the herb of healing, the pipe of peace, and the blossoming red stick. Each of these gifts presented to him, began with the west, then the north, the east and the south. Toward the end of his vision, the Grandfathers gave the same gifts as before. In addition, as each Grandfather spoke he melted down into the earth and rose again. This suggests we are born of the earth, and in death, we will return to the earth as a circle of life, and then start the whole process over again.

Black Elk:

The fifth Grandfather, the oldest of them all said; *Grandson you have seen all things of the universe. You will return to the natural world with power, for on earth hundreds will be blessed and hundreds will be ablaze! Observe!*

Clarification:

The oldest Grandfather, the Great Mystery, makes the statement: 'Hundreds will be blessed; hundreds will be ablaze.' This statement represents a matter of choice each person will make with respect to walking the 'red' or 'black roads.' Does one work with the light or with darkness? If a person works with courage, impartiality and love, to name a few, the positive will enlighten them (light), hundreds will be blessed. If a person works with fear, prejudice and hate to name a few, the negative will consume them (darkness), hundreds shall be ablaze. This suggests that at the end of the fourth ascent, not everyone will see the light. It also shows there will be balance between positive and negative forces on earth.

Out of darkness, fear, prejudice, hate, and anger, many people will be ablaze does not necessarily have any reference to Hell. The traditional Lakota person does not believe in a place called Hell. They understand negative-thinking people are 'consumed' by their own negative thinking. Remember, when walking the 'good red road', we simply borrow the emotional tools from both positive and negative forces. We then return these tools, when finished with them, staying in spiritual balance. Remember, what we put out into the world, we get back, so do no harm.

Black Elk:

Black Elk looked down and saw his people, they were all happy but there was a boy lying in a tepee looking dead whom he recognized as himself. The oldest Grandfather sang a song that went like this: *There is a boy lying in a sacred way, in a sacred way he lays. In a sacred way, I made him walk.*

Clarification:

This song states the Great Mystery placed Black Elk's earthbound body into a state of suspended animation with his family, while his To'wakaŋ was with the Six Grandfathers in the spirit world, experiencing this vision.

Black Elk:

As the rainbow tepee began to swing back and forth as if in a wind, Black Elk exited and noticed the Morning Star rising slowly and then the sun jumped up to greet him. As he walked by himself, Black Elk heard the sun singing a song as it slowly came into view.

Clarification:

The time for Black Elk to return to his earthbound body and family was drawing near; the rainbow tepee built and roofed with clouds began to break up. Daylight began to break the darkness and the earth came into view. Black Elk saw the Morning Star appearing. For many years, people have asked me if the Lakota worship the sun as a god. I just reply the sun is an essential relative or ally (spirit); it is not a god to the Lakota. Life could not exist without the sun's energy for greening and warming the earth. The traditional Lakota greet the sun every morning, offering thanks and gratitude for its being there. With this comes wisdom and knowledge as they seek the light of understanding.

Black Elk:

Black Elk was feeling lonely when a voice above said; Look behind you! When he looked up, he saw the spotted eagle floating over him. He looked to where the rainbow tepee had been and now he saw only a tall mountain located at the middle of the earth.

Clarification:

The spotted eagle would be an ally to Black Elk for the remainder of his life. Black Elk's To'wakaŋ was now seeing into the natural world, as the spirit world slowly faded behind him. The tall mountain would be Harney Peak in the Black Hills.

Black Elk:

Black Elk was alone now, with only the spotted eagle hovering over him. As he walked, he saw his people's village and saw his father and mother tending to a sick boy that was himself. As he entered his own tepee, he heard someone say, "The boy needs some water he is waking up."

When Black Elk was awake, he felt sad that his parents did not realize where he had been.

Clarification:

The reunion with Black Elk's earthbound body and his To'wakaŋ is not so unique. Many people, including myself have reported the same feelings of seeing their bodies as they begin the out of body journey, and again upon their return. The mind is a powerful tool when we learn how to apply it.

Out of Body Experience

On February 6, 1973, I moved from Gainesville, Georgia back to San Antonio, Texas to take a job as a design engineer. Barbara, a girl I was dating, remained in Georgia to settle our affairs, and planned to join me in Texas when she had accomplished this. For the next three weeks, she would make one excuse after another as to why she could not join me. This was creating some confused feelings within my life, as I did not understand why she was stalling. On March 5, 1973, at 9:30 pm, I began one of my deep meditations while sitting on my bed with the intent of getting some answers as to what was going on between Barbara and me.

With no idea, as to how I was going to accomplish this, I decided my need to know what was going on, was greater than any doubt regarding my ability to create an "out of body experience". Before long, I began to experience an incredible light feeling, I felt myself floating around the room. When I looked down, I saw myself sitting on the bed and then began moving toward the window. Floating through the closed window I slowly moved forward, floating up and over the treetops. Moving faster, I gained altitude and speed, flying over the tops of buildings and trees. The distance between San Antonio and Gainesville was about 1000 miles, but it seemed to take only minutes to arrive at her parent's home.

All at once, I was standing in her parent's dimly lit kitchen, looking toward the adjoining dining room. There were soiled dishes and food containers still on the table. I could smell the cornbread, bacon, and beans; I had no sense of hearing, my vision had some sense of color, but I lacked any peripheral vision. I also had no emotional attachment to my surroundings. As I stood there, I noticed a white hue flickering through the open doorway located at the far end of the dining room. As I approached the doorway and looked through, I noticed the flickering hue was coming from their television located in the living room.

The show was Late Night with Johnny Carson. He was telling one of his jokes and laughing, but it was as if they had turned off the volume. My first thought was, 'it is too early for Johnny Carson,' as it was not even 10:00 pm. I then noticed a clock on the wall which indicated 10:40 pm - one hour ahead of Texas. Barbara's father had fallen asleep in his easy chair, and her mother Joann was sitting on the couch across the room, watching the show. As I moved into the living room, Joann jumped, looking startled and confused but then slowly returned her attention to the television.

Continuing down the hall toward Barbara's old bedroom, I realized she was not at her parent's home. Almost instantly, I found myself standing on the redwood deck located over the hitch of the trailer home we had shared. I stood, looking through the sliding glass door into the living room, and noticed Sue, a young woman staying with Barbara. She was standing in the kitchen, leaning on the breakfast counter that opened into the living room.

She seemed to be in deep thought as I entered through the closed glass door. Startled, Sue jumped back, expressing the same startled look as Joann and then slipped back into her deep thoughts.

Moving through the living room, I proceeded down the long hallway floating through the closed door of the bedroom. Barbara was sitting up in bed reading a book when she abruptly jumped, looked puzzled and confused, and then slowly returned to her book. Once I had seen her, I could not stay any longer. It was like stretching a rubber band out to its limit, and then releasing it all at once. I returned to my body with such speed and force it knocked me over backward onto my bed. My heart was racing. Out of breath, I lay there thinking, 'What the heck just happened?'

There must have been some sort of out of body experience or journey, but I could not be sure if this had actually happened. A few days later I asked Barbara if she wanted to make this relationship work or not. She said it would be best if we went our separate ways, as she needed to move on with her life. It would be early June before I would hear from her again.

Barbara and Joann were visiting family members in San Antonio when she asked if we could talk. She came over to my apartment for a short visit, and stated, "I just could not leave my family in Georgia," and apologized for the way things worked out between us.

Somehow, the conversation moved to an occurrence whereby Barbara told me that a few months earlier her mom, Sue and she thought they saw me enter rooms and then fade away. I said, back in March, while in a deep meditation, I visited each one of them, telling her where and what each one of them were doing that evening. Wide-eyed, she said it was exactly where they were and what they were doing that evening. That was the last time I would hear from her.

In the summer of 1994, while visiting Fast Horse at his home in South Dakota, he said that he could be in two places at the same time. He went on to say, "One evening last month I sat quietly in my home, and at the same time, visited friends nine hundred miles away. I was standing on an upstairs balcony looking over the rail at my three friends. When they noticed me, I walked along the rail and disappeared through a doorway."

One of these people were visiting with us that evening and confirmed that all three of them had seen him, standing on the balcony, and then disappear. Most Medicine Men know how to do this, and use their To'wakaŋ at will to create the out of body experience.

The reason for writing about Fast Horse and my out of body journeys are to show the similar experience we had within the natural world. The only difference between Black Elk's and ours is he spent much of his time in the spirit world.

Chapter 16: Butterflies of All Colors

The year was 1881, at the age of 18, Black Elk was taken to a hill by a wise old medicine man named Few Tails to lament, cry for a vision (Vision Quest). The difference between lamenting and the vision Black Elk received when he was nine years old is, when you lament, your physical body is present. When Black Elk received his vision of the blossoming tree, it was through his spiritual body, the To'wakaŋ.

The following is a summary account from John G. Neihardt's *Black Elk Speaks*, Chapter 15 Dog Vision, [University of Nebraska Press, The Complete Edition, 2014.]

Black Elk:
After Few Tails put Black Elk up on his hill to lament, he stood in the center of his circle of sacred ties facing the west and began to cry for his vision. He asked spirit to accept his prayers and help him to understand. As he stood there, a spotted eagle flew in and landed in a pine tree in the east.

Black Elk faced the north and moved toward that direction, asking spirit to accept his prayer and make him understand. Just then, a chicken hawk flew in and landed in a bush just south of him.

From the center of his circle, he turned toward the east and approached, asking spirit to accept his prayers and help him to understand. A black swallow flew all around him and landed in a tree not far off.

As he turned to face the south Black Elk said he was only trying to cry, but now he truly began crying for he was remembering all the people who have made their spirit journey. It is also the place of the peoples hoop and blossoming tree. He also remembered Crazy Horse who used to be their strength, but will never come back to help the people.

Clarification:

In the Lakota way, when one is crying for a vision they pray to the four directions, starting in the west. We repeat the same prayer to the north, east, and south. If two or three of the Grandfathers are busy with other prayers, then at least one of the Grandfathers will hear the prayer and take it to the Great Mystery. The hawk can carry the prayers to the spotted eagle, who can carry the prayers to Great Mystery (as it flies the highest). The storm-driven swallows fly ahead of the storm as an early warning to all things; the thunder being nation is coming. When Black Elk faced the south, he thought about all his people that had made their spirit journey. The south is where we begin our earthbound journey, and at the end of life, we return to the south where we begin our spirit journey.

Black Elk:

As Black Elk cried, he noticed a dust storm coming upon him from the south. When it was close, he saw it was a swarm of butterflies of every color. They circled around him in such force and numbers he was unable to see anything else.

The spotted eagle spoke to Black Elk and said; *Observe these people, they are yours, and you will help them, for they are suffering greatly.* As he stood in silence, he thought he could hear the butterflies making a sobbing sound as if they were crying as well.

Clarification:

The butterflies represent the transformation of the two-legged people of all colors. The spotted eagle was telling Black Elk to help the two-legged people of all colors come together as one people- a repeat of his boyhood vision when he saw horses of many colors. One important point

I need to make is, if this vision had only been about the suffering of the Lakota, then the butterflies would have been all red, and the same would apply with the horses - all red.

Black Elk:

The butterflies turned and all flew back toward the south when just then the chicken hawk spoke; *Your Grandfathers are coming from where the sun goes down, listen you can hear them.* Black Elk looked up and saw the thunder beings coming out of the west making thunder with streaked lightning.

As Black Elk stood in the darkness, he saw two men coming out of the clouds. When they were close to the ground, he noticed a dust cloud rising upward and around the dust, he saw the heads of dogs peeking out. He then noticed the dust was the same butterflies he saw earlier, now swarming around the dogs.

Clarification:

One of the many teachings I received was: when we go into a sweat lodge, one sprinkles cedar leaves onto the heated stones, thereby invoking the power of the thunder being nation, as the cedar tree is a companion to the thunder beings. The reason for the sweat lodge is to purify the soul and remove all negative emotions, as the thunder beings will consume the negative. If a person were to hold onto fear, the root of negative emotion, then fear itself would most likely drive the person out of the lodge, as all negative energy cannot stay.

The dust storm that turned out to be the swarm of many colored butterflies with heads of dogs peaking out of it fits nicely, as most dogs cannot be trusted alone with a juicy piece of meat. The reason the Lakota kept the drying racks high off the ground was to keep the dogs from getting at the dried meat, as they would consume it all, leaving the Lakota with nothing to eat; sort of like the wasichu, taking everything of value and leaving little for the Indian people. The swarm of many-colored butterflies is symbolic of the people of every color coming together in the fourth ascent to expose the wasichu for their greed and pilfering of the land. History has shown that out of chaos knowledge and understanding is born.

Black Elk:

At this point, the two men mounted sorrel horses marked with black lightning and dove down upon the dogs with their bows and arrows. The butterflies changed into swallows, diving and turning about the two riders.

The first of the riders dove down and ascended with the bloody head of the dog on the point of his arrow and the second rider repeated the same as the thunder nation cheered them. When the two men ascended together the heads of the dogs changed into the heads of wasichu. Soon the vision finished and the storm came incredibly loud and frightening.

Clarification:

The two men riding sorrel horses were the embodiment of the thunder beings. The color red (sorrel horses, copper-red) represents purity and the color black (streaked with black lightning) represents the thunder beings. They were coming to purify the land and remove the wasichu that are acting in a negative way. The butterflies that changed into a swarm of swallows, swooping and whirling amongst the great storm, represented the warning: the thunder being nation is coming. The hungry dogs represented the self-serving wasichu.

Black Elk:

Black Elk said he was afraid now as he prayed to the Grandfathers and asked the thunder nation to pity him. He said he knew what the Grandfathers wanted of him and he would do his best to accomplish it.

Surprisingly Black Elk realized he was no longer afraid and thought it would be best if they killed him, as he might have a better life in the spirit world. He lay down in the center of his prayer circle wrapped himself up in his buffalo robe and waited for the thunder beings. He could hear the sharp rain and beating of the hail all around him as the giants sang.

Black Elk said no hail or rain fell into his circle, but he could hear the rain filling the ravines around him as the voices of the thunder nation moved off in the distance.

Clarification:

The teachings say nothing will come into your sacred vision quest circle to harm you if you believe in the prayers placed into your flags and prayer ties. Black Elk had a relationship with the thunder being nation. They took pity on him and showed Black Elk how things would change if he would reach out and help all the people.

The Great White Giant of the north joined the Thunder Being Nation of the west in bringing the hail along with the rain that fell just outside Black Elk's circle of prayer ties thus, showing him their true power. As I was taught, true power lies with spirit; Medicine Men simply borrow this power through ceremony for a short period to help the people, and then release it back to spirit. I have heard many a Medicine Man state: 'I am just a hollow bone, allowing spirit to work through me.'

Black Elk:

Black Elk slowly fell asleep as it was getting late. He had a dream that showed his people in distress and some were sick. He watched with sadness when abruptly a bolt of light jumped skyward. From the place where this light jumped colorful lights shown upward touching the sky, and then they disappeared. From this place, an herb began to grow. Black Elk studied it so he would not forget what it looked like. A voice said; *Hurry your people are in need of you!*

As Black Elk stood up, the Morning Star was rising slowly in the east and in the clouds. He saw faces of newborns and the people waiting to be born. There were stars glowing in all colors, with people mingling below, birds were singing and horses whinnying happily with the sounds of deer and buffalo off in the distance.

Without warning, he was startled by the sound of someone saying, "Wake up, it is time to go!" Black Elk thought at first it was a spirit, but realized the voice was that of Few Tails coming for him.

Clarification:

Again, as in his great vision when he was nine years old, the sight of sad, troubled and sick people was not as much about physical problems as it was representative of a people without a spiritual way of life. In this dream vision, Black Elk saw the herb he would use on the earth, for the earth is where his power is. He saw smiling faces of babies and people yet to be born, which suggests in the future things would get better for his people, all his people.

Black Elk:

Black Elk went with Few Tails back to where they had the sweat lodge and purified him in the hot steam. Afterwards some wise old men sat and asked Black Elk to speak of what he had experienced. After smoking the pipe together, he told them everything, and they instructed him to perform his vision for the people. The old men said it would be a dog vision and he must use the Heyóka to make the people laugh.

Clarification:

When Few Tails came for Black Elk, they returned to his camp where he held his pipe out to the six directions, starting with the west, next the north, the east, the south, the up, and the down. As with all vision quests, when Black Elk had done this, they went into a sweat lodge and after the purification ceremony, they smoked his pipe. He then shared his vision with some wise old men. They instructed Black Elk as to what he was to do with respect to this vision.

When a person has a vision, they must act on it, making it a part of their life. Because his vision was of the thunder beings, Black Elk would have to perform the dog vision for the people, using Heyókas to make the people laugh, as laughter in itself is a healing for the Niya.

At nineteen years old, he found an herb with blossoms of four colors: a blue, a white, a red, and a yellow, and used it when he performed his first healing. He received it from spirit as his medicine to represent the four-blossoming herb of his vision. I have never seen such an herb nor has anyone else I know of. As with gifts from spirit, sometimes these gifts are only for the person receiving the vision. Black Elk would have carried the four-blossoming herb in a medicine bundle, away from curious eyes.

The Pipe and Butterflies of Every Color

In the early summer of 1990, an extraordinary and mysterious event occurred to Kathy and me while traveling through the Black Hills of South Dakota. This would be the second time in two years I would take my pipe to Bear Butte to pray with it. What made this trip different is I felt a strong desire to enter the ceremonial side of the Butte, the rocky eastern side. I noticed the ceremonial encampment did not have any tents or sweat lodges set up, so I knew I would not interfere with any vision quest or other ceremonies that take place on Bear Butte. I proceeded to work my way up the rocky Butte until I came to a small flat area facing west.

My friend did not want to encroach on my need to pray and smoke the pipe, so she found a spot along the path where she could pray in her own way. Before setting the pipe out, I introduced myself to this area of the Butte and asked if it would be okay to be here. I then began to set items out from my pipe bundle when I noticed two men far off, standing in the south of the ceremonial encampment below. One of the men was pointing toward where I was sitting, when a strong wind unexpectedly appeared from their direction, blowing the leather bag of caŋśaśa over, and spilling it onto the rocks. I began picking up the caŋśaśa and placing it back into the leather bag and then threw some out to the Butte stating, 'I have come to this place to pray with this pipe and I feel a strong need to be here; forgive me if I am out of line.'

As the wind began to settle down, I reached for a pinch of Caŋśaśa and prepared to add my first prayer to the pipe when I noticed a large dust cloud in the southwest moving up the Butte toward me. As it drew closer, I noticed it was a large swarm of butterflies of all colors. They swarmed all around me and then turned toward the northwest as they flew back down the Butte. I sensed the spirits approval, and then continued to fill the pipe and pray. After smoking the pipe, I began to work my way back down the hill to where my friend was sitting on the trail.

She said that she was in the middle of her prayers when a bee stung her. She went on to say, "I was thinking, 'is this a good or bad thing to happen when on the Butte?' Just then, a bunch of butterflies of all colors began flying all around me." Looking perplexed she said, "what do you think the meaning of this is?" Smiling, I told her how these colorful butterflies had just swarmed around me earlier, while filling my pipe.

That day on Bear Butte, we thought it represented some type of acceptance for Kathy and myself. I had not had the opportunity to finish reading *Black Elk Speaks*, so I was unaware of his dog vision and the butterflies of every color.

This was my first encounter with these butterflies. As of this writing, I have not experienced this strange event again. I am convinced what Black Elk saw and spoke of in his dog vision was 'butterflies of every color'.

Today the deeper meaning for me is connected to my vision of 1973 when spirit said; *You will pick up the peace pipe (caŋnuŋpa) and seek out/or go to the Lakota to learn how to carry it. When you learn how to carry the pipe in the traditional way, you will begin to teach people how to reverse the negative.*

The butterflies of every color represent the transformation of human-kind coming together as one from the four directions. By embracing the sacred hoop of the people and stepping off the 'black road' and back onto the 'red road,' they (the people) choose to reverse the negative.

Black Elk:

As Black Elk cried, he noticed a dust storm coming upon him from the south. When it was close, he saw it was a swarm of butterflies of every color. They circled around him in such force and numbers he was unable to see anything else.

The spotted eagle spoke to Black Elk and said; *Observe these people, they are yours, and you will help them, for they are suffering greatly.* As he stood in silence, he thought he could hear the butterflies making a sobbing sound as if they were crying as well.

Chapter 17: Spirits and the Lottery

It was Saturday, February 22, 1992, around 6:00 am. I woke to the sounds of birds scolding a squirrel that lived in the large tree outside my bedroom window. I was hoping to be able to sleep in as I had worked late Friday evening, but the squirrel messing with the birds put that hope to rest. As I laid there with my eyes closed, thinking of all the ways I could rid myself of the annoying critter, the thought of Mitakúye Oyasin crowded the idea out, for he was just being a squirrel.

It was apparent I was not going to get back to sleep when all at once, I found myself standing in a room with my friend, Kathy. She had just won a lot of money on a lottery ticket and had reinvested some of her winnings. She was standing in front of a pick-four machine with a bouquet of twenty's, ten's and five's and a few lotto tickets clutched in her left hand. She then pulled the lever on a pick-four machine and began checking the new tickets. She began laughing, saying, "I won again." Then unexpectedly, I was back in my bedroom, with the squirrel outside my window, still annoying the birds. It was strange and extremely confusing, as I knew I had not fallen back to sleep.

Later that day, I met up with my friend and told her about the strange vision of her winning the lottery. She said that would be fun, I should try it someday. We both needed to do some shopping, so she rode with me to get some items at a pharmacy. Afterwards, we went next door to the supermarket.

At the checkout, Kathy remembered my vision and asked if I had a few bucks she could borrow. I gave her two dollars and she bought two lottery tickets. As we were driving away from the store, she began scratching at the ticket, one line at a time, only to discover the first ticket was a dud. After scratching the second ticket she began yelling, "I won, I won," something she always says, even if it was for just one dollar. She kept saying, "Go back, I want to cash this in." so we turned around and she cashed in the ticket for $100.00. She wanted to buy some more tickets with her winnings and asked how many she should buy. Remembering I was only watching her in the vision, I said, "You need to make that decision on your own."

She bought twelve more tickets and then walked over to the pick-four machine to try her luck there. I could not keep from smiling as she stood in front of the machine with a bouquet of twenty's, ten's, and five's, and a few lottery tickets clutched in her left hand.

On the way back to my apartment, she began scratching off each ticket. She came across three free tickets, two $2.00 winners and another matching game ticket worth $50.00 dollars, all from the same store. Analogical skeptics might pass this off as purely coincidental, which of course, is their problem.

Clarification:

This chapter gave me the opportunity to discuss the To'wakaŋ in more depth. I experienced a future event, taking place on the same day, the déjàvu effect. Normally when I experience déjàvu, I remember the event as a dream. On this day, I was in a trance like state and saw my friend standing in front of a pick-four machine holding her winnings.

I believe spirit was showing us how the To'wakaŋ functions, even if this event had no real importance to our life's journey, it was a fun experience for the both of us.

Chapter 18: The Shortcut

It was late in June of 2005. A group of six friends requested a trip to the sacred sites in the Black Hills. My wife Ginger and I had made this trip together many times over the past five years, and were comfortable bringing people of good intentions along. Our first site to fill and smoke our pipes would be at our camp near Keystone. The following day we headed for Bear Butte where we filled and smoked our pipes. That evening the group asked if they could visit Needle's Eye after dark.

We were planning to leave around 9:30 pm, but a storm blew in, requiring us to break down the kitchen canopy before leaving. One of our friends wanted to petition me with his pipe as a request for some teachings, so he went off to fill his pipe. Time seemed to be slipping away as a light rain fell, and it was getting late, around 10:30 pm. After some time, the young man presented his pipe to me and said, would you teach me about the Lakota spiritual way of life?

I took his pipe and explained: "I am not a Medicine Man or spiritual leader, as an elder I will agree to help you understand these ways and will not exceed my knowledge." He agreed to these terms as he reached over to light the pipe.

Upon the first draw, the pipe plugged up, preventing me from smoking it. I handed his pipe back to him with his first lesson: "Always make sure your pipe is cleaned after each use, before you do anything." I went on to say, "If you do not take care of the pipe, it cannot take care of you." I instructed him to remove his smoking mixture, place it into the fire, and then clean his pipe. I told him he should refill his pipe and present it in the morning, as it was getting late. By the time, he finished cleaning his pipe, it was about 10:50 pm, with a light rain falling.

Some people within the group were questioning whether we should still plan on going, as it was late and still raining. I remember saying, "Time is not a factor and as for the rain, it will not be a problem tonight at the site." I do not know why I said that, it just seemed like the right thing to say at the time. One of the women decided not to join us, she said she was tired and wanted to get some rest. With light rain falling, seven of us set out for Needle's Eye in a 15-person van.

The trip would take us through Keystone, past Mount Rushmore on Route 244, to Highway 16 toward Custer, and Route 87 toward Sylvan Lake. On Route 87 we came upon the steep grade and the four switch backs, entered the narrow tunnel before reaching the Ranger Station located by Sylvan Lake, and then on to Needle's Eye. Due to the size of this large van, it took us about fifty-five minutes in the dark of night to arrive at Needle's Eye.

When we exited the vehicle, the rain had stopped and the sky was clearing. Everyone moved into areas of personal interest, and made their own requests to be at this place. After Ginger and I had made our request, she asked me to join her on a walk through the tunnel. I was a little surprised, as it was an extremely dark night and the tunnel was even darker. Ginger insisted she needed to make the walk and would be careful, so I agreed to go with her. As we made our way through the dark tunnel, we kept to its center prepared to use the flashlights only if a car should enter.

The first thing we noticed were colorful little lights dancing about in the tunnel. When we exited the far end of the tunnel, we stood on the road, looking back at the entrance into the circular parking lot from whence we came. As we proceeded on our return trip down the long dark tunnel, the little lights began dancing along the walls. We noticed the entrance into the parking lot was beginning to glow, as if someone was shining a light at the entrance. As we drew closer, we saw what appeared to be an energy field running up and around the edge of the entrance way.

This energy field consisted of tiny specs of colorful light shimmering as it moved up and over the edges of the entrance. (See Figure 10 and 11)

When we stepped into the circular drive, we noticed the stars had lit up the entire area, and all the granite monoliths had come into view. Our small group had spread out throughout the parking lot, absorbing the entire energy of the place. Ginger suggested that two people at a time should experience the tunnel and then turn around to see if they saw the same energy field at its entrance. Four out of five people saw the colorful energy field immediately. The shimmering colorful lights at the entrance of the tunnel, reminds me of Black Elk's description of the tepee roofed with clouds and a rainbow as its open door.

I can still remember the summer night of 1996 when a voice said; *This is where we brought Black Elk.* For me, this is the earthbound location of the rainbow tepee. Who could have guessed this place has so much to offer in the spiritual sense, with these tourists and their children climbing all over these Grandfathers (granite monoliths). Somehow, I think the Six Grandfathers do not mind the noise of children's laughter, as they must like having their children, all their children of every color, so close to them.

When we decided to head back to our campsite, it was 1:15 am. As we prepared to head north on Route 87, the group began discussing their experiences at the site. We had only been driving for about ten minutes, when we came upon a sign that read, "Highway 16 ahead." As we pulled up to the intersection, everyone began saying, "What happened to the tunnel and four switchbacks?"

We turned right onto Highway 16 and then right onto Route 244 toward Keystone. During the drive, I began explaining that in 1996 Devin and I experienced the same phenomena whereby we did not encounter the tunnel or the four switchbacks. In the time, it took me to explain this phenomenon, we came upon a sign that read, 'Mount Rushmore ahead'.

When we arrived at our campsite, Ginger looked at her watch and said, "It only took us twenty minutes to make the return trip." Looking back at

Devin's and my experience the evening of June 1996, with respect to this same time warp, it began to make some sense to me, if that is even possible under these circumstances.

In Late June of 1996, Devin and I made the trip to Needle's Eye after 12:30 am and returned to our campsite in Keystone after 2:00 am. In Late June 2005, Ginger, our friends, and I began the trip to the 'needles' at 10:45 pm, drove the four switchbacks and the narrow tunnel at the top of the rise and it took us fifty-five minutes. On our return trip, it was 1:15 am; we did not encounter the tunnel or the four switchbacks, and the trip took only twenty minutes in the dark of night. The only conclusion I can draw from this is, both the 1996 and 2005 trips took place in late June and this phenomenon occurred after midnight, not before.

Now, as a design engineer, I was having a hard time with this one. I had to figure out how this could have happened, so I opened up Google Earth on the computer and focused on Route 87, Highway 16, and Route 244. I noticed Harney Peak is located between Route 87 and Route 244. I printed a copy of the photo; using a compass. I scribed an arch from Harney Peak through intersecting points on Route 87 and Route 244. What I found was the compass intersected large portions of Route 87, which included the narrow tunnel and the four switchbacks, a large portion of Route 244 just before Mount Rushmore and all the Needle's Eye parking area.

I believe something is going on with respect to Harney Peak on certain times of the year and after midnight when few people drive the dark roads of the Black Hills. What I know is this phenomenon happened to my friends and me, twice. Once in 1996 and again in 2005, and there are no other roads we could have taken. As of this writing, I have not experienced this phenomenon in the Black Hills since. Perhaps, it has something to do with the time of year, positions of the planets or, a special gift.

Figure 10: Viewed from the parking lot, looking east into Needle's
Eye tunnel.

Figure 11: Looking in the direction of the west, from inside the Needle's Eye tunnel. Colorful energy field moved up and over edges of the opening.

Chapter 19: Mitakúye Oyasin and the Flowering Tree

The way I was taught, in the beginning of time, Wakáŋ Táŋka Tuŋkášila summoned four spirits (angels to some) to stand in the four directions and listen for all the peoples' prayers. Wiyóhp̓eyata Tuŋkášila (Grandfather of the West, the first spirit) agreed to this and established the western direction. Waziyata Tuŋkášila (Grandfather of the North, the second spirit) agreed to this and established the northern direction. Wiyóhiyaŋp̓ata Tuŋkášila (Grandfather of the East, the third spirit) agreed to this and established the eastern direction. Itókaǧata Tuŋkášila (Grandfather of the South, the fourth spirit) agreed to this and established the southern direction.

In doing this, Wakáŋ Táŋka created the four cardinal directions: the west, north, east, and south. Wakáŋ Táŋka (the fifth spirit, the oldest of them all) would listen for the prayers from the "up" position, the sky. Tuŋkášila Maká (Grandfather Earth, the sixth spirit) or Unci Maká (Grandmother Earth) agreed to listen for the prayers from the "down" position, the earth. In doing this, the spirits established the six directions. The people, all the people; two-legged, four-legged, six and eight-legged, winged, and rooted ones alike, established the seventh direction, regardless of where they are located within the universe.

The best example of the seventh direction can be explained in this manner: if you hold four toothpicks so they each point to one of the four cardinal directions: (the west, north, east and south,) then add two more toothpicks, one pointing up and one pointing downward, you end up with something resembling a child's jack. At its middle is the center of the nation's hoop, the seventh direction, it is the point where all six directions meet, the dwelling place of the Great Mystery. If we do not walk in a spiritual way, we abandon the seventh direction causing it to breakup, fall apart, and then the flowering tree dies.

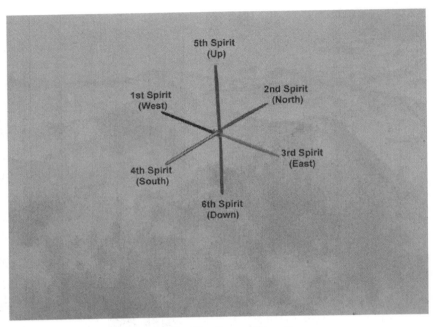

Figure 12: The Seven Directions

The seventh direction is the glue that holds the six directions together. By releasing one's grip on the toothpicks, it represents the abandonment of the seventh direction and the toothpicks break up, fall to the ground, and the tree dies.

Fast Horse spent over six years talking with me about Mitakúye Oyasin. I would just sit quietly, listening to all his teachings, without asking any questions. He moved in and out of different subjects with respect to the Lakota spiritual way of life, inserting the concept of Mitakúye Oyasin as he spoke. It took me the better part of a year to understand how and why Fast Horse kept repeating these teachings, finishing with a summary of Mitakúye Oyasin. Traditional Lakota use a circular narrative in their story telling, repeating the heart of the subject several times within the story before returning to the beginning. The western method uses the linear narrative of storytelling, having a beginning, middle, and an end.

Remember, Mitakúye Oyasin is one of the more important statements in the Lakota language; it is a state of being, not above or below but a relationship with all things. One does not assume they are more important than, say, a red ant or a tree.

If you see the red ant or tree as a relative and treat them with respect, you might open a channel of communication. For example, if you entered a room with several people and if you had knowledge that would improve their lives, would you share this information with them if they said you were an ignorant bubble-head.

If you chose to share this information with them, would they even hear you? Chances are they would not.

If you entered the same room with several people and had knowledge that would improve their lives, would you share this information with them if they said you were extremely knowledgeable. If you chose to share this information with them, would they even hear you? Chances are they would. It is just that simple. Treat all things with respect and a channel of communication can easily open to you, Mitakúye Oyasin.

The Pet Housefly

It was early in the evening of October 1993; I arrived at my home and began to prepare supper when I noticed a small housefly buzzing around the kitchen. My first thought was, it is October, why is this fly still around? I retired into the living room where I could watch the news and eat my supper, when I noticed the fly landing on the back of the couch, a couple of feet from me. I reached for a newspaper and began rolling it up with the intent of putting this fly out of my misery. I was taking careful aim to

161

smack this little fellow when I heard a voice say; Do not hurt that fly. I set the paper down, studying the fly and wondering why the spirits were protecting it.

If I had to put up with this fly for a few days, then maybe I should share some of my supper with it. I walked back into the kitchen, set out a small paper plate and added a little of everything from my plate. The fly flew into the kitchen and proceeded to feed at the small plate. As I was returning to the living room, my thoughts were, 'This is a strange way to set out a spirit plate.'

A spirit plate consists of a small portion of everything that makes up the meal. This is a traditional ceremony for honoring the spirits of the food, and any spirits present in the room; it is the Lakota way of giving thanks. Within a few minutes, the fly returned to the living room and flew to the same spot on the couch, a couple of feet away from me as if it too were watching the television.

After about four hours of putting up with this new-found roommate, I retired to the bedroom, only to have the fly follow me. It landed on the top of the headboard and just sat there looking at me. I laid there thinking, 'this fly had better stay off my face tonight.' When I woke up in the morning, the fly was still on the headboard. I took a quick shower, fixed breakfast, and remembered to add something to the spirit plate. The fly landed across the counter and proceeded to feed at the plate, staying away from my breakfast plate.

Believing this house-guest would only last a few days or at most a week, I continued to put out the spirit plate at each meal. What was odd is this funny little fly followed me around the house like a pet dog or cat. When I arrived at home from a long day at work, the fly would buzz around, dipping and rolling as if it were excited to see me then, settle down at the same spot on the couch.

The strange behavior of this fly continued, not for a couple of days or even a week or two- it went on from October to November, December,

January, February and well into March. Over the many months of observing this fly, I began to look forward to this strange relationship as this fly continued to act as if it were happy to see me and did not behave in the obnoxious manner most houseflies exhibit. One evening when I arrived home, I did not notice the fly buzzing around. After a couple of days, I figured it must have exited the house looking for a girlfriend or boyfriend. At the time, I had no idea as to how to determine the boy/girl thing, so I just called it, Little Fly.

Two weeks had passed when my friend, Kathy came into town for a visit. I was having friends over for a pipe ceremony and feast, so she was helping straighten up the house. She was about to dust off a 12-inch-tall Franklin Mint, a fine porcelain figurine of a Medicine Man called the Spirit of the Sioux. The figurine was bare-chested with a buffalo robe wrapped around his waist, wearing a buffalo horn headdress supporting a single trailer of 44 eagle feathers. He was in a dance position, with a rattle clutched in the right hand held low to his right knee. He held his left hand high above his head, clutching a short eagle claw staff.

Kathy looked over at me and said, "I found your pet fly." The fly was located on the clutched left hand of the Medicine Man as if he had reached up and grabbed the fly out of the air. The fly had expired in the grasp of this porcelain figurine and remained in that position for a little over two weeks before my friend discovered it. I felt a little sad thinking this little fly never had the opportunity to be with its own people. The fact I shared my apartment for around five months, developing this rather odd friendship with a housefly, caused me to take a hard look at the true meaning of Mitakúye Oyasin.

It is my belief this housefly came into my life to help establish the foundation of a relationship with all things. What I learned was that standard houseflies only live for 15 to 25 days. In optimal conditions, they can live for two months. I guess my apartment and daily spirit plate made this optimal at best – up to five months. My other thought was maybe this was a spirit and not a fly at all, but then why does that matter. After all, we did establish a unique friendship. I did not have a funeral for the little fellow, but I did place it in a nice flowerbed, out of respect for its teachings. Keep in mind, Mitakúye Oyasin is the cornerstone of Black Elk's great vision, and this little fly expressed the depth of this relationship.

The point worth making here is when spirit said; Do not hurt that fly. Had I ignored the voice and swatted it with the newspaper, I would have missed out on this extraordinary relationship and a valuable teaching.

I believe if people exhibit an interest in learning about the Lakota spiritual way of life, there should not be any pressure to either step onto the 'red road' or stay away. When given proper teachings, a person can make better decisions as to their spiritual needs. I thank the Six Grandfathers and the good people of the Lakota nation for accepting me when I came home after being away for so long. Four generations is a long time to be away from the Lakota spiritual way of life. Through the people's teachings and kindness, it has cemented my place on the 'good red road.'

The 'red road' is a hard and long road; it is not easy to find your way along this path. Over the years, I have witnessed many people, both Indian and non-Indian alike, begin the walk, and after a few years step off the 'red road', looking for something else to fill their spiritual needs. I believe people are searching for answers as to who God is. My role in all this is not to compel people to join me on the 'red road', the Lakota spiritual way of life, but to speak freely with those seeking true spiritual understanding.

One point I would like to make here is the great religious doctrines of the world have some similarity with one exception: the Lakota spiritual way of life is not dogmatic. Lakota traditions change with the passage of time, and each family looks at a same tradition in a slightly different manner. What is important to understand, is the main body of a ceremonial tradition remains in place, with small changes accruing between the spirits and the ceremonial leaders working within the traditions. A traditional person would state, 'I was taught to conduct ceremony this way', and would not say, 'you are wrong for doing the same ceremony in a slightly different manner'.

Black Elk:

Black Elk stood on the highest mountain of them all (Harney Peak) and looked down, he saw the hoop of the nation, and it was made of many hoops of his people spreading out wide as the day and the stars. At its center was the blossoming tree, to shade all people of one father and mother, and he knew it was sacred.

Clarification:

With this single statement, Black Elk sets the stage for the world to come together, while embracing each other's differences, creating one circle, wide as the day and the stars, made of many hoops of his people, all his people. This will take place when we, the people of the world, stop finding fault with each other's ethnic and religious differences, creating many hoops that make one circle wide as the day and the stars.

On one of our trips to the Black Hills, Ginger and I escorted a group of five people to the sacred sites. On the last three days of our week-long excursion, we camped at a KOA across from Gray Horn Butte. We had gained permission from the park ranger to pick a small amount of single stem sage from the field adjacent to our campsite.

While kneeling in the field and picking the sage I heard a small voice say, "What are you doing?" Looking up, I noticed an elderly woman standing on the opposite side of the fence. In her frail voice, she asked again, "What are you doing?"

"We are picking sage to use with our ceremonies, as sage displaces all negative energies," I said. She seemed pleased at what she had heard, thanked us for the lesson, and then bid us farewell.

Figure 13: Devil's Tower. Lakota refer to it as Gray Horn Butte (Pahá lie ptehé hota), or Bear Lodge (Mato Tipi). Conventional view from southern direction off State Hwy. 24.

Figure 14: This is the reason the Lakota call Devil's Tower, Gray Horn Butte. This is the non-conventional view of Devil's Tower, viewed from the northern direction off State Hwy. 24

~~~

Later in the day, we set off walking the pathway that wrapped around Gray Horn Butte, when we came across the same elderly woman walking with a friend in the opposite direction. She stopped and asked, "Where are you going, and what are you carrying in the bundle?"

"This is a sacred pipe and we are taking it onto the west side of the butte to put up some prayers," I said. She looked at us with a big smile and asked, "When you pray with your pipe, would you remember my family and me! When I go to my church, I will pray for you and your family."

The point in writing about the elderly woman's comments was to show how people could support each other's spiritual differences. She did not attempt to change our spiritual walk by degrading our religious beliefs. On that day, the elderly woman prayed for us in her way and we prayed for her in our way. What is important to remember is, on that day we each prayed to the same creator using different languages to say, God.

The following is a summary account from John G. Neihardt's *Black Elk Speaks*, Chapter 25, The End of the Dream, Black Elk ends with this statement:

Black Elk:

Black Elk said when he looked back from his old age he could still see the women and children massacred in the ravine at Wounded Knee as if it had just happened. He felt something else died that day: the people's vision died and was shattered. It was a wonderful vision. He felt he was a sad old man, and had done nothing with his great vision. He said the hoop of the nation is gone and the sacred tree has died.

Clarification

Black Elk's vision has not ended, when given the vision of the sacred hoop, and the blossoming tree, Wakáŋ Táŋka said Black Elk would see four ascents that were generations. In chapters 10, 11, 12, and 13, I explained the timeline for each of the four ascents. On the first two ascents, the people walked the 'good red road', the spiritual road. These roads were not extremely steep, lasting thirteen and fifteen years respectively.

On the last two ascents, the people walked the 'black road', the road of difficulties and war. These roads were much steeper, lasting forty-eight years for the third ascent and as of 1939 through to the present time; we are still on the fourth ascent. In 1931, Black Elk said we were close to the summit of the third ascent and said the fourth ascent would be horrible.

The following is a summary account from John G. Neihardt's *Black Elk Speaks*, the Authors Postscript, Black Elk sends his last prayer from Harney Peak.

Black Elk:

Black Elk stood at the top of Harney Peak holding his pipe in his left hand and dressed in his red long johns. With outstretched arms, he sent his prayer to the Six Grandfathers. Tears ran as he spoke aloud stating the tree did not blossom and he has turned away and done little for the people. He said I stand at the top of the world where you took me as a young boy and instructed me, for I am just an old man now and the tree is dead.

He went on to say that this might be the last time he remembers the great vision they gave him. He asked the Great Mystery, if any part of the root lives, then nurture it that the tree may bloom with birds singing amongst the leaves. He asked the Great Mystery to hear his prayer, not for him, but for his people that they might find the 'good red road' once again. He stood with tears running and addressed the Six Grandfathers saying, "O make my people live."

Figure: 15: Black Elk standing on the summit of Harney Peak. As of August 2016, Harney Peak was renamed, Black Elk Peak.
Courtesy John G. Neihardt Trust, Western Historical Manuscript Collection-Columbia.

Clarification:

In all fairness to Black Elk, the blossoming tree will not bloom until we finish the fourth ascent. He could not stop what the people of the world would be going through during the third and fourth ascents as predicted by Wakáŋ Táŋka; the whole world will experience complete chaos as they travel upon the 'black road' of the last two ascents.

In Black Elk's great vision, he spoke of dropping the Morning Star herb of understanding onto the earth. Where it touched the earth, it took root and sprouted four flowers on a single stem, a blue, a white, a scarlet, and a yellow; and these colors shot up into the sky, replacing darkness with light, and all living things saw it.

By Black Elk sharing his great vision of the sacred hoop and blossoming tree with John G. Neihardt, and allowing him to place it into the book *Black Elk Speaks*, he was dropping the Morning Star herb of understanding onto the earth. In doing this, Black Elk planted the seed that will bring the blossoming tree back to the center of the nation's hoop.

Black Elk knew John G. Neihardt was coming to speak with him long before he showed up for the interview. Neihardt's connection to this vision is as mysterious as the vision itself. Neihardt seemed driven in seeking out Black Elk for a story that would reach to depth of his soul and change him, his family and the world's way of thinking for generations to come.

Black Elk:

Through a naming ceremony, Black Elk gave Neihardt the name Flaming Rainbow. He believed Neihardt was a "word sender." Black Elk said the world is a garden, and Neihardt's writings are like rain, making the garden green. After his writings cross over the earth, the understanding of his words will remain in the west like a Flaming Rainbow.

Clarification:

It is my belief that when the four main colors of humankind come together, black, white, red, and yellow, from the four directions and stand at the center of the nation's hoop, they will represent the seventh direction and are the embodiment of the blossoming tree. All of us make up its leaves and blossoms. When we lose, or abandon our spirituality, we are no longer connecting with the center of the nation's hoop; we, the leaves, begin falling from the tree of life, and then it dies, along with our connection to Great Mystery.

There is still time for the Great Lakota Nation to rise to the occasion, bringing the blossoming tree back to the center of the nation's hoop for all the people. It is time for those who seek knowledge and wisdom to look for the light of the Morning star. It is with this intention that one seeks the light of understanding and not the ignorance of darkness.

If the great Lakota Nation does anything with Black Elk's vision, I pray it will be to go out into the world and share this great vision with the people, not to convert them to the Lakota spiritual way of life, but to teach the concept of Mitakúye Oyasin. By embracing each other's wonderful differences, we can become one people of one father and one mother. I believe the concept of Mitakúye Oyasin can enhance any religious doctrine without having to make any changes to the doctrine. When the world learns to embrace Mitakúye Oyasin, then waging war on each other will become a little harder to accomplish.

Please understand, I am not a Pollyanna type-person who thinks the world will find perfect love and peace; there are always going to be people who are filled with fear, anger, hate, and darkness. What is important is people can become more aware of everything around them, not out of fear, but out of understanding and wisdom. The choice is there for all of us. Do we work with light or with darkness? It is time to step off the 'black road' of the fourth ascent and onto the 'good red road'. Some visions can take a lifetime to realize such as, 'reversing the negative.'

In the early spring of 2013, I began writing this book. It was forty years from the date of my first vision, which suggested I would pick up the "pipe," learn to carry it in the traditional Lakota way, and then begin to help the people 'reverse the negative.' Over forty years ago, spirits woke me up and gave me the vision that would lead to the writing of this book, *Mystic Visions: Black Elk's Great Vision Clarified.*

When a person receives a vision, they must act on it, living out their lives and bringing the vision to full fruition. To not act on one's vision, is to reject it in its entirety, and deny the spirit that brought the vision to you in the first place. In retrospect, be careful what you ask for, you may have to live with it for the rest of your life.

Black Elk would make his spirit journey on August 19, 1950, six years after I was born. The Six Grandfathers told Black Elk he would see four ascents that were generations before he made his spirit journey, and my generation is the fourth. When Black Elk spoke of the Great Vision and Flowering Tree with John G. Neihardt in 1931, he was 68 years old and five feet, eight inches tall. When I began work on this book in 2013, I was 68 years old and five feet, eight inches tall, a funny little coincidence, seriously, I do not think this has any real meaning, although it can be a little fun thinking about it.

In closing, one important consideration within Black Elk's Great Vision is: not one time did spirits say to Black Elk, the Lakota people would travel upon the two roads of the four ascents. They said; *Your people* would travel upon the two roads of the four ascents, the words *your people*, represent all things within the universe. Remember the butterflies of every color; Black Elk's vision is for the entire world, not just for the Lakota, it is for all his people.

In March 2016, a petition to canonize the Holy Man Nicholas Black Elk was presented to the Catholic Diocese in Rapid City, South Dakota.

Over 1,600 signatures were presented to the bishop of the diocese asking him to nominate Black Elk for sainthood. For years, Black Elk served as a Catholic catechist, serving Lakota people living on the reservations.

Two miracles attributed to Black Elk would have to be proven before the pope could declare him a saint. If the Catholic Church needs miracles, all they would need to do is, read *Black Elk Speaks* by John G. Neihardt. The book is full of miracles, and his selfless act of service to the people of the world.

Black Elk could balance his love for the Lakota spiritual way of life, as well as, follow the teachings of Jesus through the Catholic Church. For Black Elk, how he chooses to pray to spirit is not all that different.

Through the writings of John G. Neihardt's *Black Elk Speaks*, Black Elk's Great Vision will survive within the hearts of the people throughout the world who may choose to live through its teachings.

Mitakúye Oyasin!

END

Appendix 1: Suggested Reading

Black Elk Speaks, by John G. Neihardt, University of Nebraska Press The Complete Edition, 2014. This book, offers a historic look into the life and Great Vision of the Holy Man Black Elk an Oglala Lakota.

Black Elk Lives, Conversations with the Black Elk Family, by Granddaughters, Esther Black Elk DeSersa, Olivia Black Elk Pourier; and Great-grandson's, Aaron Jr. and Clifton DeSersa; Edited by Hilda Neihardt and Lori Utecht, University of Nebraska Press, 2000.

Black Elk & Flaming Rainbow, a book filled with memories of Hilda's days with Black Elk, his family and her father John G. Neihardt, by Hilda Neihardt, University of Nebraska Press 1995.

The Sacred Pipe, Black Elk's account of the seven rites of the Oglala Sioux, by Joseph Epes Brown, University of Oklahoma Press. 1989

Bury My Heart at Wounded Knee, by Dee Brown, Bantam Books 24th Printing 1976.

The Lance and The Shield: The Life and Times of Sitting Bull, by Robert M. Utley, Ballantine Books, a Division of Random House, Inc. 1993

How to Take Part in Lakota Ceremonies, by William Stolzman, Tipi Press, St Joseph's Indian School, Chamberlain, SD, 2004

Blue Water Creek and the First Sioux War 1854-1856, by R. Eli Paul, University of Oklahoma Press: Norman, 2004

Appendix 2: Lakota and French Word Meanings

A-hey, a-hey: Used in prayer to call for spirit power

Até Wakáŋ Táŋka: Father Great Mystery, God, the fifth Spirit

Caŋśaśa: Smoking mixture for pipe, Lakota word for the inner bark of red willow

Caŋnuŋpa: Peace pipe

Cekṗa: Twin, the placenta, connection with nature

Déjàvu: A French word having the sense of, "I've been here before

Haŋbleceya: Crying for a vision, lamenting, or vision quest

Hehaka Sapa: Black Elk

Heyóka: The contraries or clowns, jokers

Hoka Hey: Used to rally the hunters; to start an attack; to make ready; to draw others attention.

Hunkpapa: Those who camp at the end of the horn

Huŋḱápi: Making of a relative

Iktómi: Spider, the trickster

Inipi: Purification ceremony (sweat lodge)

Ishŋa Ta Awi Cha Lowaŋ: Coming into womanhood

Itazipacho: Those without bows

Lakota: Teton Sioux, western band of the Sioux

Maká Iná: Mother Earth the sixth spirit

Mato Tipi: The Bears' Lodge, a.k.a. Devil's Tower

Miniconju: Those that plant by the water

Mitakúye Oyasin: We are all related or, all my relatives, a relative to all things

Naǵî: The guardian, aura

Niya: Breath of life, heart/mind/lungs

Oglala: To scatter one's own

Oohenunpa: Two kettles

Pahá lie ptehé hota: Gray Horn Butte, a.k.a. Devil's Tower

Śiyó: Prairie Hen

Sicangu: Burnt thigh, (Brulé, French, meaning burnt thigh)

Sihasapa: Blackfeet or black sole, not to be confused with the Blackfeet of Montana and Canada

Sioux: French for the Dakota, and Lakota

Tapa Waŋká Yap: Throwing of the ball

Tatanka Ska: White Buffalo

Tióśpaye: Extended family

To'wakaŋ: Advanced guardian, top of head

Tuŋkášila: Grandfather a term showing respect

Tipi: Tepee a conical tent

Wiyóhpeyata Tuŋkášila: Grandfather of the West, the first spirit

Wazíyata Tuŋkášila: Grandfather of the North, the second spirit

Wiyóhiyaŋpata Tuŋkášila: Grandfather of the East, the third spirit

Itókaǧata Tuŋkášila: Grandfather of the South, the fourth spirit

Wakáŋ Táŋka Tuŋkášila: Great Mystery, God, the fifth and oldest spirit of the sky

Maká Tuŋkášila: Grandfather Earth the sixth spirit

Uncí Maká: Grandmother Earth the sixth spirit

Unhee: An interjection expressing surprise

Waǧa Caŋ: Cottonwood tree

Wakíyaŋ: Thunder Beings

Wakíyaŋ Oýate: Thunder Being People

Wanáǧi: Ghost

Waŋblí Gleška: Spotted Eagle

Wasichu: Non-Indian people, fat takers

Wicasa Pejúta: Medicine Man

Wicasa Wakáŋ: Holy Man

Wiwaŋ'yag Wachi'pi: The Sun Dance

Yuwipi: Binding Ceremony of the Medicine Man

About the Author

Quentin H Young was born to Rosemary Likens Young and Mayo Beckford Young. His mother's side of the family has Lakota (Sioux) Sicangu (Brule) lineage; his father's side is Welsh.

From the Lakota lineage, his grandmother's name was Rose Leaf Eliot, (see Figure 1) and his great grandmother was named Eliza Milton, (see Figure 2) a full blood Sicangu Lakota borne in 1854 in Nebraska. In 1855, a soldier took Eliza from the battlefield of the Blue Water Fight and gave her to the Milton's, a white family from Missouri who later adopted her. My mother believed the reason her grandmother, Eliza, named her daughter Rose Leaf and why Rose Leaf named her daughter (my mother) Rose Mary, was due to their knowledge that the Sicangu were located on the Rosebud Reservation. It was their secret way of connecting with their Lakota Sicangu roots.

Quentin has been involved in the Lakota spiritual way of life since 1950 at age 6, by 1989, he began keeping a caŋnuŋpa (pipe). In 1996 Quentin became a Sun Dancer, and has danced consecutively for twenty-one-years

Quentin served as paratrooper in the U.S. Army's 101st Airborne from 1962 through 1965. He retired as a design engineer after 30 years. During this period, he designed and developed a complete set of prison locking devices for three corporations within the United States. Today, many of his lock designs are in use throughout the United States, Canada and Mexico.

Quentin lives in Illinois with his wife, Ginger, he has two grown children, two grandchildren and Sapa, his black cat who sat on the desk the whole time watching him write this book.

~~~

If you liked Mystic Visions: Black Elk's Great Vision Clarified, please leave feedback.

You can email Quentin H. Young with your questions and comments at mysticvisions26@aol.com

Made in the USA
San Bernardino, CA
18 May 2018